OVERCOMING
CRISIS

BOOKS BY MYLES MUNROE

AVAILABLE FROM DESTINY IMAGE PUBLISHERS

Overcoming
CRISIS

the SECRETS *to* THRIVING
in CHALLENGING TIMES

MYLES MUNROE

DESTINY IMAGE® PUBLISHERS, INC.
P.O. Box 310, Shippensburg, PA 17257-0310

*"Speaking to the Purposes of God for This Generation
and for the Generations to Come."*

This book and all other Destiny Image, Revival Press, MercyPlace, Fresh Bread, Destiny Image Fiction, and Treasure House books are available at Christian bookstores and distributors worldwide.

For a U.S. bookstore nearest you, call 1-800-722-6774.
For more information on foreign distributors, call 717-532-3040.
Or reach us on the Internet: www.destinyimage.com.

ISBN 10: 0-7684-3052-6
ISBN 13: 978-0-7684-3052-3

For Worldwide Distribution, Printed in the U.S.A.

4 5 6 7 8 9 10 11 / 13 12 11 10

Table of Contents

Preface

What do you do when everything you trusted in collapses? How do you prepare for a sudden change in life? How do you recover when life hits you on your blind side? After a lifetime of hard work, dedication, commitment, and loyalty to a chosen career, how do you suddenly change your vocation and skill sets? What do you do when a lifelong dream and investment is suddenly taken from you through no fault of your own? How do you bounce back after institutions that were expected to protect you suddenly pull the rug out from under your life? What do you say to your family when you face the reality that you may no longer be able to fulfill their expectations for security, support, and provision?

Where do you go when you want to work but there are no jobs? What do you do when your sense of pride for personal accomplishment is dashed in the fires of survival? How do you go on after the legacy of years of work is erased by a pink slip from the company you helped build? How do you face the family you once left to find your fortune and chase your dreams and ask them to take you back in because your world has evaporated? Where do you go when the ones you go to for help are also in need of help?

All the above questions are actual situations I have encountered in counseling hundreds of individuals who have fallen on difficult times in their lives. Though each situation was unique, one common factor linked them all: every trying situation was initiated by what we call a *crisis*.

Each one of us will face some type of crisis. We all encounter situations over which we have no personal control, which we did not expect or could not prevent. Many of us, perhaps, are still trying to recover from a broken marriage, the stillbirth of a child, the unexpected death of a spouse, child, or loved one. Maybe you lost your dream house, your dream car, your baby, or your business. Whatever your situation, these are all categorized as crises.

Living on earth requires that we must expect the unexpected and prepare for the unforeseen. It's the nature of life. But many of us do not possess the necessary mental, emotional, psychological, and spiritual tools to successfully and effectively weather these seasons of turmoil. If this is your state, then this book is for you or for a loved one who needs to know that there is life after crisis.

Introduction

The world is in crisis. However, in the past there was no such concept as "global crisis." *Globalization* is a modern term that describes the collapse of the many barriers between nations such as distance, culture, trade tariffs, and access to global communication. This new international phenomenon began with the advent of modern travel, increased with the invention of radio, television, and telephone technology, and then exploded with the emergence of computer and cyberspace technology. These inventions have forever changed life on planet Earth as we know it, impacting the movement of people, international trade and commerce, immigration and migration, cultural interaction, and political collaboration. The most important result of this global transformation is the interdependence of nations. The reality of this new age is the fact that the circumstances, events, or major changes in the social, political, economic, and cultural environments of one nation affect the environment of many other nations and communities.

At the writing of this manuscript, the world has entered into one of the most critical international crises of our generation. Every news broadcast gives us more information about the latest financial downturn or collapse. Everybody is affected in some way, even the wealthiest people. Nobody can stop it.

Suddenly, every country in the world has entered into a recession—or worse. Unemployment rates are soaring. Homeowners are facing foreclosure. Businesses are facing bankruptcy and liquidation.

The economy of my country, the Bahamas, depends heavily on tourism. Guess what will get slashed first from people's budgets when money gets tight? Ninety percent of our jobs in the Bahamas are built around tourism, and that means our entire economy gets rocked when the stream of tourists becomes a trickle because of an economic recession/depression. (Ironically, Cuba used to be the number one tourist destination in our region before the Cuban government turned socialist during the prolonged crisis of the Great Depression—which means that it was an economic downturn that allowed for our success as an alternative island vacation spot.)

Meantime, ongoing wars and rumors of wars are decimating cities and nations, adding to the "normal" level of crime and human degradation across the globe. On videotapes and in photographs, the faces of anguished refugees appear so often that most people have become used to seeing them. In the past, we hardly ever talked about terrorists, but now you can hear that word every day of the week.

Completely beyond our control, natural forces also threaten human welfare. At any given time, something is happening somewhere in the world: hurricanes, typhoons, tornadoes, earthquakes, mudslides, tsunamis, droughts, floods, famines. The list goes on and on. People are always in some kind of a crisis.

We are vulnerable. We are very fragile. As the world's economies are imploding, fear is exploding. Fear is defined as a lack of confidence, and fear itself feeds the recession. When consumers lose confidence in the system, they stop participating in it. They stop buying things. Consumer confidence is vital for the success of the capitalist economies that most of us live in because everything in a capitalist economy is built on people's buying and selling. When buyers stop buying, the sellers have to stop selling. Incomes dwindle and accumulated wealth does too. The fear itself does not dwindle, though. It grows.

Crisis is not too strong a word for what is happening. We are walking through a worldwide crisis, and most of us are (or soon will be) walking through significant personal crises as well. Many of our personal crises will be related to the broader crisis. If you have a job, you may lose it. If you own a business, you may have to pull back and find new strategies for making it through this difficult season. If you are a pastor or a missionary, you may find yourself short of funds as people can no longer contribute money to your ministry.

On top of that, surely you will have your ordinary level of difficulties to deal with. You may have health problems, marital problems, family problems. Sometimes, if you stack a financial disaster on top of your existing problems, it's just too much. You will be in high-alert crisis mode before you know what happened to you.

The purpose of this book is not to frighten you, nor is it to report breaking news, nor is it to bemoan the wretched state of the world. The purpose of this book is to give you some practical advice.

I didn't think it up. I'm just the messenger for the One who has the answers to every catastrophe. When even the experts don't know what to do, it is time to hook up with Someone who is smarter than all the experts put together. When you need to overcome a crisis, it is time to look to the Overcomer.

You must understand that *the Kingdom of God is never in crisis.* Let that sink in. The Kingdom is never in crisis mode because the King is bigger than any crisis that has ever happened, will ever happen, or is happening right now. He knows what to do.

Not only does He know what to do, but also He cares for us, both individually and corporately. He loves people. And God has never failed His people yet. The important thing is to make sure that you are one of His people.

This book is about how to make sure that you are walking according to His principles as a citizen of His Kingdom. It will help you hold up a measuring rod to your current situation, and it will show you how to measure up to His righteous standards so that you, too, can overcome every crisis. Then you can turn to help your neighbor on the way. If you claim citizenship in the Kingdom of Heaven, you have a way out of every crisis.

Notice that I did not promise you a crisis-free life. No, I promise you a way out, a way to overcome each crisis, whether big or small. Nobody is exempt from crises, including Christians. You *will* have crises. Jesus said, "...In this world you will have trouble. But take heart! I have overcome the world" (John 16:33).

What is your crisis right now? As you allow Him to convert your crisis into an opportunity for growth and grace, you will be able to bring a little more of the Kingdom of Heaven to this disillusioned, worn-out world.

CHAPTER I

Global Crisis, Personal Crisis

Seeds of faith are always within us; sometimes it
takes a crisis to nourish and encourage their growth.
—*Susan Taylor*

What constitutes a "crisis"? How bad does a situation have to be? What kind of crises have you been through in your life? What kind of crisis are you in right now?

It is true that what can seem like a crisis to one person is not a crisis to someone else. Yet for everyone, a crisis is an event over which one has no control. Crises are experiences that you did not anticipate or prepare for. They take you by surprise, and they fill you with anxiety.

Let's say the weather forecast says that a hurricane is coming. Here in the Bahamas, we know that could be serious. We know that when hurricanes hit, they don't mess around.

Suddenly your priorities are different. If you were planning to go visit your friend, you change your plan. If you have a family, you try to make sure they will be safe. You do whatever you have to do to get ready for the storm before it hits your neighborhood.

Or say the doctor says, "You've got three weeks to live if you don't change your habits." He is not joking. All of a sudden, you get motivated to change. This is a crisis. You may not be able to avoid all of the consequences of your eating habits, your smoking, or whatever, but you will probably clean up your act. You will stop eating cheesecake and macaroni salad on the same plate, and you will start eating raw carrots. You may have been trying to stop smoking for 50 years without success, but now, instantly, you will stop cold turkey.

A crisis forces the issue. You cannot control the crisis that has come upon you, but you can begin to control some of the details of your predicament. You can make some headway against it. Later on, you may even be able to appreciate the crisis for forcing you to change. (One thing I *like* about hurricanes is that they clean things up. All the rotten trees, the poor construction, the junk lying around—the hurricane comes through and creates a mess. But five months later, the mess has been cleaned up and you see a cleaned-up landscape, new flowers, new buildings.)

Effects of a Crisis

Jesus said that we will always have troubles (see John 16:33). One crisis after another will come our way as long as we live, regardless of how well-insulated we try to make ourselves. So it is important to get a grip on how to overcome not only some of the circumstances, but also—especially—our emotional responses to difficulties. If we can regain our emotional footing in a storm, we will be able to overcome. First, before we can regain our emotional footing, we need to put our feet on the Rock-solid foundation of God.

A crisis produces some or all of the following emotional responses in us:

- Fear
- Trauma
- Depression
- Despair
- Frustration
- Anxiety
- Loneliness
- Worry
- Hopelessness

We can be consumed by any of the following states of mind:

- A sense of abandonment
- A sense of loss
- A sense of death
- An urgency for survival

Being fearful makes people respond in a knee-jerk fashion to a crisis, and they may set up a cycle of negative consequences, such as the following:

- Abuse (physical, psychological, verbal)
- Crime
- Domestic violence
- Substance abuse

These reactions set people up for further crises. You probably know what I mean from experience.

The Experts Cannot Help

This fast-spreading economic disease called "recession" may be causing many of our personal crises—or adding to the crises we already have. Some commentators, early in the financial crisis of the fall of 2008, began to use the more frightening word: *depression.* Very often, an economic depression causes personal depression. One crisis piles on top of another.

The systems of the world's kingdoms are collapsing. The world is filled with fear. Powerful people are wringing their hands. The leaders do not know what to do. They are, as I heard Mr. Gordon Brown, the prime minister of Great Britain (and an economic specialist) say, "experimenting." A lot of decisions are being based on theories rather than experience. We do not know yet if the experiments will work. Nobody has faced this exact kind of a crisis situation before.

The world economic system is spinning out of control. Powerful people are powerless to stop the breakdown. The relatively manageable problems of the recent past now make those times look like "the good old days." Now it is too late to go back to them.

The Blame Game

The prevailing tendency is to blame somebody or something. "Whose fault is it? Let's go get 'em." But that does not help, does it? Anyway, there is really no one person or event to blame. When you get laid off from your job, you want to blame the management or the company. You want to counterattack and hold someone responsible for your dilemma. I tell you, do not waste your energy on that, especially these days. The whole world is in a crisis, and you just happened to have gotten knocked off your horse too.

When the United States Congress asked a spokesman for the Federal Reserve what caused this meltdown, his answer contained a very biblical word: *greed*. He said that when the people in charge become greedy, they plant the seeds for the collapse of the very economic system they think they can use to their advantage.

What is greed? Greed is the mismanagement of resources for personal benefit, coupled with a disregard for the benefit of others. Greed is when you want more than you need at the expense of everybody else. Greed means I know I need only one pillow, but I want ten. I need only one little plateful of food at a time, but I want the whole restaurant.

Greedy people don't care who gets hurt. They just go after whatever they want and don't concern themselves with other people. They see an opportunity to acquire more money, greater status, or further pleasures, and they charge ahead in pursuit of their selfish goals, regardless of how many people they have to trample on in the process.

Right now people in the United States are losing their homes by the thousands. Foreclosure is taking about 3,000 homes a week away from families who usually have no other place to go. Some of them will end up living in their cars. At this writing, it is estimated that by the end of 2009, over 2 million homes will have been lost. Just a handful of greedy people have caused a tidal wave of grief for others.

Greed walks hand-in-hand with partners such as malice, deceit, theft, envy, evil thoughts, lewdness, adultery, slander, arrogance, murder, and all kinds of folly (see Mark 7:21-22). The reason these evils travel together is because all of them originate in the sinful hearts of human beings. In many ways, they represent aspects of greed. Theft is greed for things that are perceived as valuable to the thief. Envy and slander represent a greed for reputation. Lewdness and adultery are forms of sexual greed. Arrogance and murder amount to greed for power and vengeance.

In this parable about the rich but foolish farmer, Jesus gave us His advice about avoiding greed:

Then He said to them, "Watch out! Be on your guard against all kinds of greed; a man's life does not consist in the abundance of his possessions." And He told them this parable: "The ground of a certain rich man produced a good crop. He thought to himself, 'What shall I do? I have no place to store my crops.'

"Then he said, 'This is what I'll do. I will tear down my barns and build bigger ones, and there I will store all my grain and my goods. And I'll say to myself, "You have plenty of good things laid up for many years. Take life easy; eat, drink and be merry."'

"But God said to him, 'You fool! This very night your life will be demanded from you. Then who will get what you have prepared for yourself?'

"This is how it will be with anyone who stores up things for himself but is not rich toward God" (Luke 12:15-21).

Watch Your Heart

"All right," you might say, "so we can blame the economic mess on the greed of the fat cats in high places. What good does that do me as I stand in the unemployment line?"

For one thing, it can be a caution to you. Do not take the same path yourself. Do not let your own financial uncertainty make you do something rash and foolish. Do not do something dishonest. Do not go the way of the world. Do not worry about yourself. Instead, put your trust in God and ask Him what to do. He knows what to tell you. He's just waiting for you to stop trying to solve things yourself and to start to pay attention to His directions.

If you pay attention, you will know when He is pricking your conscience. He will warn you when your heart starts to brew up some form of malice, deceit, theft, envy, evil thoughts, lewdness, adultery, slander, arrogance, murder, or other kinds of folly.

When Jesus said "watch out," He meant that it could happen to you, especially if you do not even know you're greedy. Here you are, driving to work in your used car. You pass someone's shiny new car. You do not need a new car. Your old car is working fine, and it is paid for. What are you going to say?—"Oh, the Lord is gonna bless me with a new car." What makes you think that would be a blessing? You don't need any new car. If you get one, you're going to have to go into debt. You call that a blessing? God calls it a debt. The car you already have is good enough. Next time you go somewhere in it, take Jesus' advice: "Watch out! Be on your guard against all kinds of greed; a man's life does not consist in the abundance of his possessions."

I will never forget the day I went to visit the late John Templeton, who had a house in the Bahamas in a beautiful place where the wealthy people live. I walked into his office. He greeted me with a smile, and he kissed me. In front of me I saw this old man in worn-out shorts and tennis shoes with holes all through them. He had on a bush jacket that was ragged because he had worn it so much. Here was one of the wealthiest men in the world, dressed like that. Mr. Templeton of the Templeton Foundation, worth billions of dollars, gave me a tour through his little office. That office was so small I could hardly find a place to sit as he talked with me.

This man was giving away more than a million dollars every year to people who had contributed something exceptional to the world's understanding of God. The Templeton Prize had been given to extraordinary individuals such as Mother Teresa, Billy Graham, Aleksandr Solzhenitsyn, Chuck Colson, and Bill Bright. But Mr. Templeton did not appear to fit the part. His clothes were all worn out, and his office was no bigger than the back room of other offices.

I thought to myself, *If this guy was a Bahamian, he'd be wearing snake leather shoes, an alligator belt, and a tiger shirt.* But I think he had his priorities straight. He was so wealthy partly because he gave away so much. I think he took Jesus' words seriously: "Give, and it will be given to you..." (Luke 6:38).

Crisis Forces Development

Too much of the time, by default, people let their greed rule their decisions. They do not think about what they are doing. Down the road, their greedy decisions result in a crisis. In a crisis, not only do other people get hurt, often the greedy ones do, too.

When things reach the crisis point, there is only one way out, and it has to come through some kind of shift or change. Certainly, you cannot keep on going the way you have been going. Usually you no longer have the same resources anymore. Times of crisis usually reveal how well or how poorly we have managed our resources. Now you will be forced to change your ways, hopefully for the better. This is the "silver lining" of a crisis.

Crisis always forces development. It creates the opportunity for creativity. It provides a powerful motivation to change. You have to invent new ways to deal with old problems. If you are a national leader, you have to collaborate with others to develop a new economic system. If you are an ordinary person with ordinary job qualifications, you have to start fresh with some new ideas. You have to push aside your regrets about the past and your instincts to be angry and to blame somebody else for the pickle you are in. You *have* to. In order not only to survive but to thrive, you must do something new.

Here in the Bahamas, with so much of our national economy dependent upon tourism, we have to diversify. That does not mean that "somebody else has to diversify." That means a lot of us have to diversify. This economic crisis shakes the foundations of what you thought was traditionally sound. You need to look around you and see what kinds of needs are going unmet. Can you start a business to meet those needs? Our oceans are full of seafood. If somebody from right here in the Bahamas does not start to make better use of all that seafood, some enterprising person from China will soon take advantage of it.

This is also true of every other nation. The need to find new ways and develop new products and services is imperative in the midst of crisis.

What kinds of resources do you already have? Do you have a car? Do you have a house? Do you have a computer? Think about some way you can not only make a living, but do it in a way that doesn't trample on others. Without being greedy and hard-hearted, you can find a way to do an honest day's work and provide for your family.

You will often hear it said that the words for *crisis* in Japanese and Chinese are the same as the word *opportunity*. There's wonderful truth in that. You wouldn't think that those two words have anything in common until you realize that the seeming defeat inherent in every crisis holds the keys to an unanticipated victory. When the atomic bomb was dropped on Hiroshima at the end of World War II, it obliterated the city. Over a hundred thousand people are estimated to have been killed. The buildings were leveled. The soil was poisoned. But the Japanese people took hold of the hands that reached out to help them, and they worked day and night to rebuild their city and their country. You know what happened. Now they are number one in so many categories: their cars, their electronics, and a lot more.

You see, if you think this way, every disaster gets turned in a new direction. Your crisis becomes your best opportunity. If your house burns down, you don't despair. Instead, as soon as you can, you seize this opportunity to build a new and better house. If you get laid off from your job, you either find a better one, or you create a better one by going into business for yourself. Out of your crisis comes your opportunity.

If you call it an *opportunity* instead of buckling under the load of the words *crisis* or *tragedy or disaster,* then you can start taking advantage of what has happened. You stop thinking of yourself as somebody who lost a job and start thinking of this as the first time you have been set free from a job. Now you can do something new!

The rest of the world will continue to wallow in all those results of a crisis: fear, trauma, depression, despair, frustration, anxiety, loneliness, worry, hopelessness, a sense of abandonment, a sense of loss, a sense of death, an urgency for survival, abuse, crime, domestic violence, and substance abuse.

But not you, because you are not under the world's system. You will rub shoulders all the time with people who are anxious and afraid. You will hear people express how lonely they feel, how they feel as if they are the only ones having such big problems. They will get more and more desperate, while you and everyone else who does it God's way will be busy stepping up on top of your problems to get a better view. Once you really step up on them, you can see much farther than you could see before. The air is better up there.

The Bible says you should be anxious for nothing, but in all things pray and never stop praying:

> *Do not be anxious about anything, but in everything, by prayer and petition, with thanksgiving, present your requests to God. And the peace of God, which transcends all understanding, will guard your hearts and your minds in Christ Jesus* (Philippians 4:6-7).

Instead of worrying, rejoice. "Rejoice in the Lord always. Again I will say, rejoice!" (Phil. 4:4 NKJV). Do not throw away your confidence. He who began a good work in you will finish it. (See Philippians 1:6.) You do not have to wait for Heaven. What you are going through right now is only a test. And, I promise you, there is an abundance of life after the test, right here on earth.

Tested and Approved

God has given us a foundation (Himself, His Word), and He will always supply a strategy if you ask Him. Inevitably, your crisis situation will force you into supplication. You will apply to Him for the supply you need. You will learn that He wants to supply you with far more than simple relief from your difficulty, as desirable as that may be. He wants to supply you with Kingdom riches in the form of wisdom, peace, and faith.

I will keep on reminding you of this: Kingdom citizens are not immune to crisis. It is important to remember this. Just because you are living in God's Kingdom does not isolate you from unexpected, uncontrollable events. When a storm hits, it will hit everyone. Hurricanes don't go around the homes of believers to target only the houses of nonbelievers.

Jesus made this point when He spoke about building your house upon a firm foundation of His Kingdom Word:

Everyone who hears these words of Mine and puts them into practice is like a wise man who built his house on the rock. The rain came down, the streams rose, and the winds blew and beat against that house; yet it did not fall, because it had its foundation on the rock. But everyone who hears these words of Mine and does not put them into practice is like a foolish man who built his house on sand. The rain came down, the streams rose, and the winds blew and beat against that house, and it fell with a great crash (Matthew 7:24-27).

The violence of the storm hit both of the houses. The one that was built on the rock was hit just as hard as the one that was built on the sand. Hurricane-force winds lashed sheets of torrential rain and rising floodwaters threatened to finish both houses off. The crisis affected everybody.

The difference is in the response of each of the houses. The one that was built on a strong foundation could stand up to the winds and the rain. The other one collapsed. Jesus wants us to know that *survival will depend on your foundation knowledge.*

Remember, He said that anyone who hears His words and puts them into practice will be like a man who built his house on an immovable rock. In contrast, anyone who does not put His words into practice will be like a foolish man who builds his house on the beach or on a sand dune. If you don't build on the right foundation, then you have a problem.

The storm is the test. It is a crisis, and crises are going to happen. But it is not the storm that is the problem. The problem is the difference between how the houses respond to the storm, and that depends upon how they were built in the first place.

It's too late to remedy the problem when you're in the middle of the crisis. But you can learn from it and do better next time. Gather up the pieces and consult the Master Builder before you rebuild. God wants you to learn how to obey Him in everything. Your life depends on it.

Palace to Prison

You can decide how obedient you will be, and you can grow in your obedience as you grow through your life. Even if you get thrown into the deepest dungeon as Joseph was, you can land on your feet at the end. We'll look at Joseph some more in the next chapter, but for now let's just look at how he made his foundation strong.

His story is very familiar to us, and it can give us a good example of how to live. (The story is found in chapters 37 and 39–47 of the Book of Genesis.) Starting when he was just a boy, Joseph was 100 percent dedicated to God. This did not mean that he was preserved from problems. He faced one crisis after another. In fact, it does not seem fair. It seems to me that he had more crisis situations than the "average Joe" does.

His jealous older brothers threw him into a deep pit, wanting to kill him. He was delivered from the pit by being sold as a slave to the Midianites. Slavery is better than death, I suppose, but not by much, especially compared to what he was used to as the pampered, favorite, youngest son in a well-to-do family.

The Midianites took him to Egypt where young Joseph's lot seemed to improve, at least for a while. Now instead of being a favorite son, he was the favorite slave in the household of the captain of the guard, Potiphar. He conducted himself with integrity. His conduct demonstrates that his life was still planted solidly on its original, firm foundation.

However, Joseph's integrity did not preserve him from the next crisis. In fact, his integrity precipitated the next crisis. He refused the advances of Potiphar's wife, she falsely accused him, and Potiphar had him thrown into prison. Egyptian prisons were awful places. Did he waste time blaming other people or God for his predicament? Did he sit there in the dark, plotting some kind of revenge?

No. There again, he proved his merit. He saw needs, and he endeavored to meet them. He was not afraid of hard work. He tried to make the prison better. Before long, he was helping the prison warden to administrate the place.

In the prison, Joseph met the baker and the cupbearer of Pharaoh, for whom he ended up interpreting dreams. Eventually his dream-interpretation ability led to his release, when the pharaoh had a frightening dream and needed somebody to interpret it for him.

At this point, one line of the story stands out to me. Joseph had been brought before Pharaoh, and he was interpreting the dream for Pharaoh, point by point. The dream was predicting that there would be seven years of good crops followed by seven years of drought and famine. Joseph said to Pharaoh, "The reason the dream was given to Pharaoh in two forms is that the matter has been firmly decided by God, and God will do it soon" (Gen. 41:32).

God had showed Pharaoh two times that famine was coming, to underline the fact. "The matter has been firmly decided by God, and God will do it soon." There was going to be a crisis, definitely. No use praying that it would go away. The crisis would not skip over Egypt. An equal-opportunity crisis was going to hit everybody, and God's warning had been sent so that the leader of the country would have time to prepare for it.

Prison to Palace Again

Egypt was an agricultural economy. A time of famine represented an economic crisis of the highest magnitude. Today, the United States and the rest of the Western world have industrial and technological economies, and people tend to put their trust in money. Suddenly, financial assets have been devalued, and accessible money is in short supply. You could call it a money famine.

Most of us do not hold governmental authority, but we can interpret the signs of the times. Wherever you live and whatever your position in worldly terms, do not bother to pray for this crisis to vanish, because it won't. Even fasting and praying will not make it go away. The matter has been firmly decided by God.

God is quite aware of the global economic confusion. He probably orchestrated it just to remind the capitalists that they cannot capitalize on anything. Do not blame the devil, even though the devil is involved. God probably decided to send this crisis so that people would lose faith in their false god named Money. When money is your god and your money gets devalued, your god gets devalued. Then the real God can get back on the throne in the hearts of many people.

Suddenly Joseph found himself back in a position of authority in Egypt, administrating the relief measures that were required by the famine. God orchestrated that. Joseph said, "Look, take the good years and invest them and store them up for the bad years." He was able to manage the crisis with God's help and God's wisdom. Not only did his wisdom and hard work enable the people of Egypt to survive the famine, they represented a divine provision for the survival of his own family.

In the same way, as we stay obedient to God, we will be able to weather the current money-famine or recession and all of its ramifications in our personal lives. This crisis is not a mistake.

You Can Find It in Your Bible

Every single thing that happens to you fits in with the Word of God. When Jesus says, "I have told you these things, so that in Me you may have peace. In this world you will have trouble. But take heart! I have overcome the world" (John 16:33), He is referring to your current problems. He is promising that you can have His peace in the midst of any storm. He is encouraging you to let Him help you overcome every crisis, from the everyday personal trials and tribulations to world-class calamities. He is reminding you that He is much bigger and much stronger than any crisis. He is saying that you can overcome your crisis—by following His way and by using your faith to rely on His power.

Go find your Bible and read First John 5:4 with fresh understanding: "Everyone born of God overcomes the world. This is the victory that has overcome the world, even our faith." Who is it that overcomes the unrelenting crises of the world? Only the people who believe that Jesus is the Son of God. Only the people who believe what He has told us.

Faith is believing in the dark what He has told you in the light. He has told you that He is the Son of God and that He is your Savior. He has told you that He has more than adequate wisdom and power to meet every emergency. He does not sugarcoat the situation. He doesn't say He will take you out of the world you are living in so that you can escape all of its agony. But He does make you promises. And He always comes through on them.

When I was a teenager, I read a particular line from the Bible, and it blew me away. I read this line: "God's love is long-suffering" (see Num. 14:18 KJV). It didn't say that God's love is "forever suffering." The suffering may be long, but it is not forever. By the time the "long" runs out, something will have changed. It may be you; it may be your circumstances; it may be both. Your suffering is only for a season, even if it is a long one. With His grace, you will make it through your current crisis—and through the next one after this. Because your Lord is an Overcomer, you too will become an overcomer.

Remember, the Kingdom of Heaven is never in a crisis. Our life here on earth will consist of crisis after crisis, but our foundation is in Heaven.

Chapter 2

What Does It Take to Overcome a Crisis?

I really do think that any deep crisis is an opportunity to make your life extraordinary in some way.
—*Martha Beck*

Religious people look for miracles. When a crisis comes, they want God to take care of them without any effort on their part. They are lazy. They want to find a magic supply and immediate relief from their trouble. They treat God like Santa Claus—or maybe like something less than Santa Claus because even Santa Claus says you've got to be a good boy or girl before he will bring you gifts. Religious people treat God like a genie in a bottle. If you rub the bottle three times in Jesus' name, He will come out and grant your wishes.

Kingdom people are not religious people. Kingdom people are different. Kingdom people understand how authority works. They have a daily relationship with the King. They hold the keys to overcoming every crisis that God allows to test them.

My job as a Kingdom-teaching pastor is to show you the keys of the Kingdom and to help you learn to use them. I can help you find all of the keys of the Kingdom in the Word of God. The keys of the Kingdom are the foundational truths that you need to live by if you are going to build your house on a foundation that is firm enough to withstand every storm or crisis.

What if you go to work tomorrow and your boss tells you that you have just been fired? What if your spouse opts for a divorce? What if you get cancer? With the keys of the Kingdom in your hand, you are ready for anything.

"I Will Give You the Keys of the Kingdom"

Jesus said, "I will give you the keys of the kingdom of heaven..." (Matt. 16:19). He promised to give us the keys that will make it possible for us not only to survive, but also to thrive.

Keys provide access to something. If I give you a key to my house, I have given you access to my house. I have given you a certain amount of authority and control over my house. You can step into it anytime you want to, day or night, whether I am home or not.

Notice that Jesus said, "I will give you the keys," not "a key." He will give us more than one key because He wants us to have more than one kind of access to His Kingdom. The Kingdom of Heaven operates by more than one principle. There are many ways to unlock its power.

Right after He promised to give us the keys of the Kingdom, Jesus went on to say this: "...whatever you bind on earth will be bound in heaven, and whatever you loose on earth will be loosed in heaven" (Matt. 16:19). In other words, when you take a key in your hand (one of the principles of the Kingdom), you can open or close things both on earth and in Heaven. Whatever you open on earth, Heaven will have to open for you, and whatever you lock up on earth, Heaven will lock up for you too.

You have the authority to affect decisions. When the systems on the earth are not working, banks are struggling and collapsing, people are losing their homes, workplaces are getting shuttered—it is time to take out some different keys to unlock God's provision.

Jesus also told His disciples this: "The secret of the kingdom of God has been given to you. But to those on the outside everything is said in parables" (Mark 4:11). The keys of the Kingdom are mysteries to those who do not believe. You live in the midst of a world that is confused, fearful, and frantic. God has handed you keys that He has not handed to people who do not follow Him. He has told you secrets that are going to seem like meaningless parables to other people.

This means that you have information your neighbor does not have. When the storm hits, your neighbor falls down flat under fear while you stand up and start walking in faith.

He gets all depressed while you start dancing. Both of you may have lost the same material possessions, but while he is saying, "Oh, woe! I am *never* going to recover," you say, "I know that I am going to be all right." When he says, "I'm angry about this," you say, "God allowed it, and He knows what He's doing."

You live on the same street, but your responses are very different. You are right there in the midst of the same crisis, but you are not like your neighbor. What makes the difference between you? Some basic information. You have the keys; you can unlock doors that your neighbor can only pound on with frustration.

David wrote about this in one of his psalms: "A thousand may fall at your side, ten thousand at your right hand, but it will not come near you" (Ps. 91:7). That can't happen unless you are in the midst of a raging battle. You can't experience that kind of preservation unless you are in the middle of a serious threat to your survival. That is a crisis situation. David is saying that you are going to be right in the middle of the crisis situation, that you will not be exempted from it, but that the way it affects you will be different because of your position in the Kingdom.

When you and your neighbor both find out that you have lost your jobs, you are going to have a different mentality about it. You will not go into a depression about it. You will not question God's decision to let this happen to you. Instead, you will look around, realize that you are still standing even though a thousand others lie fallen on one side and ten thousand on the other—and for that reason alone, you will rejoice.

You will not get jealous of the people who still have their jobs because you will understand that your security cannot be found in any job anyway. Your security can be found only in your identity as a son or daughter of your Heavenly Father. If you belong to Him, your position in the Kingdom is secure. It cannot be shaken. When crisis crashes in around you, you will reach into your pocket and pull out your keys.

The Number One Kingdom Key

What do the keys look like? Which ones should you pull out in order to overcome the next crisis?

The primary key—the principal principle—of the Kingdom of Heaven is this one: *management.* I call it the key of management.

The reason we are in trouble is because of *mis*management, through greed.

The only way out of the trouble we are in is through righteous and wise *management,* through God.

What is management? Here is my definition: management is the effective, efficient, correct, and timely use of another person's property and resources for the purpose for which they were delegated with a view to producing the expected added value.

Read that again, slowly and carefully. Notice the individual words: *effective, efficient, correct, timely, delegated, value.*

You must recognize the fact that you always manage another person's property, not your own property. You do not own a thing, anyway. You do not own the earth. You do not own anything that exists on the earth. You do not own the job you're going to. You do not own the business you claim as your own. You may have your name on it, but your business can be gone in one day. Whether you do it well or not, your job is just to manage it.

Every single human being is supposed to be a manager. Each one of us. When the Lord God made the earth and filled it up with resources, the very next thing He had to do was to make a manager to take care of it. Men and women were given dominion over the earth's resources. (Notice, however, that they were not given dominion over each other. God was still in charge of the people He had created.) God gave Adam and Eve dominion over the fish, the birds, the plants, and the animals. God told Adam and Eve that every fruit was there for them to eat. All they had to do was manage the Garden. God told them that the trees were good. The animals were good. The water was good. The gold was good. The resin was good. The onyx was good. (See Genesis 2:12.) God set it up so that Adam and Eve would find it good to take care of every good thing that He had created.

Psalm 115:16 reads, "The highest heavens belong to the Lord, but the earth He has given to man." The earth is the legal territory of human beings. He wants us to take responsibility for the products of the planet. God's divine goal was to extend the culture of the Kingdom of Heaven to earth.

The culture of Heaven is a culture of plenty—but only if it gets managed right. It is true that God created human beings to worship Him, but He already had plenty of worshipers in Heaven, so He did not create humans in order to obtain more worship. Heaven has always been packed full of worshipers. When God turned His attention to filling the earth with good things, He decided to create people in His own image to manage the earth.

Because God made us managers from the beginning, when He created Adam and Eve and placed them in the Garden of Eden, management (sometimes called *stewardship)* is a primary goal of the human race, whether people realize it or not. When we follow the Master Plan, we flourish. And, like Adam and Eve, when we mismanage, we lose. Although it has no effect on the management mandate of God whether we manage well or poorly, it does have an effect on how much of His Kingdom can express itself on earth.

Taking Care of Resources

Let's bring it home: when you keep coming to work late, you can lose your job. When you keep eating too much fat, you can lose your health. When you do not cultivate your friendships, they can die. If you do not keep on putting affection and respect into your marriage, it falls apart. Whatever you mismanage, you start losing. Whatever you manage properly, you protect.

Proper management applies resources in the most *effective, efficient, beneficial* way. Good managers don't waste resources, and they don't give them over to the wrong purpose. Good managers do not hoard resources, either. When you hoard things, you aren't really managing them at all. So when you earn ten dollars, you do not hoard it, but you don't spend it all on your own whims, either. You take the first dollar of it, and you give it to God. Then you ask Him what to do with the other nine dollars. That is how you *manage* your money.

Proper management is the *correct use* of something. To use something correctly implies that you will use it with integrity. You will not slip into dishonesty. If you are not supposed to use the copier at work, you will not make personal copies on it. You won't even help yourself to a paper clip. That paper clip wasn't given to you for your private use. It is somebody else's property. I know it's very small and that your boss won't miss it, but if you are managing your work properly, you will not take it home. Once you put it in your pocket without a twinge of conscience, then it is easier to graduate from a paper clip to a pencil to a stapler to a laptop computer. The principle is honesty, and that is more important than a paper clip.

Proper management is *timely use* of another person's property. (And remember that even your own property doesn't wholly belong to you.) That means you get your timing right. When the country has been plunged into economic uncertainty, you postpone remodeling your house. You change your vacation plans—unless you already live in Hawaii, you don't buy your ticket to Maui yet. You pull back. You reassess. You reorganize. You figure out what your resources are, and then you proceed to use them wisely, timing your use of them based on what you can observe and on what the Spirit of God prompts you to do.

Can God Trust You With More?

Discipline is the key to proper management. You cannot be effective, efficient, correct, timely, and beneficial to others if you do not apply consistent effort. God will give you the grace to live a disciplined life if you ask for it.

If you manage your resources well, God will trust you with more. Jesus said as much:

> *Whoever can be trusted with very little can also be trusted with much, and whoever is dishonest with very little will also be dishonest with much. So if you have not been trustworthy in handling worldly wealth, who will trust you with true riches? And if you have not been trustworthy with someone else's property, who will give you property of your own?* (Luke 16:10-12)

God will give you not so much what you *pray for* as what you can *manage*. I call it the "management of prayer." You pray for God to give you a job. God says, "OK, but the last job you had, you went to work late every day, you took two-hour lunches, you took off at five minutes to five instead of 5:30, and you lied when you said you were sick." Can you manage a new job? I wonder if you can.

You pray for a new house. God says, "What about the house you already have? Do you keep it up? I know you are only renting it, but you're not even keeping it clean."

You pray for a new car. God says, "Wait a minute. I have noticed that you do not keep your bicycle in good shape." In other words, if you are not even managing what you have now, how can you expect God to give you something bigger to mismanage?

Diligence is another key to proper management. Diligence means consistent effort too. With both discipline and diligence, you can become effective, efficient, correct, and timely. At my house, I always tell my wife and kids, "You can never be early if you leave home late." If your church service begins at 9:30, don't leave home *at* 9:30, hurrying to make it. That's late already, and it's a management problem. It's a time-management problem.

Rulership, Not Ownership

One day I was looking at the printed word *management*. I noticed something about it. I noticed that the word begins with the three-letter word *m-a-n*. Management begins with man. God gave mankind the role of management. As I indicated earlier, God gave mankind rulership, not ownership. He created everything, and He owns it all. But He delegated the management of His creation to the human race, and He calls us to account.

You're going to have to give an account to God of what you did with His money, His time, His gifts, His talents, His resources, the house He got for you, the apartment He enabled you to rent, the car you are using, and more. None of that is yours. Although you cannot claim ownership if you are the manager, your accountability comes with your responsibility to manage properly.

Don't claim to own anything. Remember that rich man in the Bible who gloated about how his hard work had made him wealthy and who decided to put up bigger barns in which to hoard his riches? (See Luke 12:16-20.) God took his life the same night. He never even got to enjoy it. He should have realized that all that abundance of provision had been loaned to him, in a sense. He was supposed to take care of it and be generous with it instead of stockpiling it and congratulating himself that all of his hard work was behind him.

Ready for Anything

Here is the bottom line. Effective management is what will determine the amount of your resources. If you are a good manager and you obey God's principles, it will not matter what kind of crisis comes; you will be ready. You will be able to weather any crisis, even if some of the resources disappear. You will have a savings account to tide you over in case you lose your job. You will know how to consider carefully whether or not you can afford to spend money right now.

Sometimes we like to quote Proverbs 13:22, at least the first part of it. The first part reads, "A good man leaves an inheritance for his children's children," and we agree with that part easily. Then we gloss over the second part of the proverb: "but a sinner's wealth is stored up for the righteous," because we're not quite sure what to do with it.

Years ago, the Lord brought me up short. I was quoting that second line as if it was a good thing to say. The Lord spoke to me and said, "Don't quote that line as if it's a good thing. It is true that wicked sinners have your wealth, but that is not a good thing." How did they get the wealth? God gave it to them. Why would He give it to them instead of to the righteous? Because they managed it better. He gives resources to those who manage well. Even if they are sinners.

That money will not come to you as you stand there saying, "Money, come!" It will not come to you by your binding or loosing anything. You may have been praying to no avail for ten years for additional monetary resources, and you still do not have a thing to show for it except sore knees. The resources do not come by prayer, even if the prayer is long and loud and sincere; the resources come through prayer in addition to good management of the resources you already have.

Start small and work up. Start by being honest, by not taking that insignificant little paper clip. Conserve. Stop and think. Do not throw away that piece of paper. Write on the back of it. Turn off the lights when you leave the room. Tithe your income. File your taxes honestly. Do not live above your means.

Economize—maximize the minimum and get the most out of the least. I was shocked when I studied economics in college and found out that when you reduce it to its simplest definition, *economics* means to maximize the minimum. You take a little and make the most of it. That is simple economics. A good manager is a good economist.

If you are an economist, a good manager, you will take one apple and plant a tree from the seeds; then, when it produces more apples, you will sell them and be able to grow more apples from more seeds. You will manage your resources so you can add value to your gift. God does not encourage waste.

If you are a mis-manager, you will take your paycheck and cash it. Then on your way home, you will stop to buy something to eat. You will notice a sign that says "Sale," and you will stop to purchase some new shoes. You will put down some more money on a new suit. What did you just do? You did not manage at all. You *consumed*. You became a consumer. Your routine is to buy, buy, and buy some more. You say, "I can get whatever I want. I have the money." Most of your paycheck was gone before your foot even touched the front step of your house.

The Proverbs are filled with good observations, such as, "...the diligent man prizes his possessions" (Prov. 12:27). The good manager values what he has already. How do you handle what you have in the rooms of your house, your money, your time, your relationships? Do you prize them? Managers prize the little things. They pick up every crumb, as the disciples did after Jesus fed the 5,000 (see Mark 6:30-44). Why did Jesus tell them to collect all the scraps in baskets? I think it is because He was accountable to His Father in Heaven, and He had just used some of His Father's fish and bread.

It can be a good idea to go through your closet and find clothing that hasn't been worn for a long time. Start wearing it again, or give it away. Take care of what you have. Manage it well. Be prudent. Be resourceful.

Another proverb reads: "The plans of the diligent lead to profit as surely as haste leads to poverty" (Prov. 21:5). This applies to people who ask for handouts. If you spend time with someone who wants a handout or something for nothing, you are in bad company. People like that are taking the easy way out, and all they will get for holding their hands out is more poverty. If you need money, you should not just ask for it. You should ask, "What can I do for you to earn some money?" Stop looking for a handout and start looking for a hand *up*. That is better management. It shows respect for the person you have offered to work for, and it shows self-respect too. It shows that you want to be diligent, to manage your efforts, and to manage your relationships.

You will find many more practical suggestions as you read the rest of this book. This is a primary principle of the Kingdom: Overcoming crisis depends on good management, and good management is the same as godly stewardship. If you live by God's principles, you will reap the increase. If you manage what He has already given you, He will be able to trust you with more.

A Test of Management Skills

As an effective manager, you will be like Joseph, whose godliness and diligence kept him within the protection of God and enabled him to draw others into the same safe place.

When you read the story of Joseph's long life, you can count many times when his management skills were on the line. They were tested. More than once, he seemed to get knocked down, but never was he knocked out. I believe that God allowed each one of those crises to test his management skills. Would Joseph rise to each new challenge? Will you and I rise to ours?

When Joseph came up against a crisis, he was quick to develop a strategy for confronting it. When he correctly interpreted Pharaoh's dream about the years of plenty and the years of famine, he came up with a plan simultaneously. He was only about 30 years old, but it was obvious to him that God wanted to warn Pharaoh of the impending crisis so that he could get his nation ready, and Joseph had already figured out what it would take to get the nation ready.

What did Pharaoh do? Thank Joseph for his suggestion, pat him on the back, and send him back to prison? Of course not. He promoted him. He said to Joseph:

> *Since God has made all this known to you, there is no one so discerning and wise as you. You shall be in charge of my palace, and all my people are to submit to your orders. Only with respect to the throne will I be greater than you* (Genesis 41:39-40).

Joseph got promoted because of the crisis, or more precisely because of his potential ability to manage the crisis. That morning he had been a prisoner in the dungeon. By afternoon, Pharaoh had put him in charge of the whole land of Egypt. Pharaoh had even given him his signet ring so that the transfer of authority would be complete. Joseph, remember, was not even an Egyptian by birth. He was a Hebrew and a foreign slave. Apparently, however, it did not matter where he came from. What mattered was his ability to manage the crisis.

So for the first seven years, he dedicated himself to traveling throughout the land while the crops were abundant. He was diligent, orchestrating the collection of all of the harvested grain, storing it up in great storehouses in the cities. At the end of the seven years when the crisis of the famine hit, the country was ready. The citizens could go to the storehouses and obtain the food they needed. They had so much that they could help the people from other countries too, and that included Joseph's father and brothers. Who could have known? Only God.

And God had prepared Joseph. By the time Joseph had to face the crisis of managing agricultural resources in the time of a regional famine, he had been prepared by having to overcome every previous crisis of his very eventful life. Each crisis had been designed by God to test Joseph and to make him more able to overcome the next crisis.

Joseph stayed close to God, even when he found himself in a pagan culture where he didn't know the language. He had always remained disciplined and careful. Unlike many of us, Joseph did not waste a nickel of his resources. He worked hard at whatever he was given to do. That did not change even when he was in the dungeon, completely out of his master's view and away from the public eye.

I'm sure he made course corrections as he went. He had a lot of time to think about what he might have done wrong and how to do better next time. He allowed God to speak to him through his circumstances. Although each test was radically different from the one before, he passed all of them. Before the onset of a crisis, Joseph was already holding the right keys in his hand, ready to unlock God's wisdom and provision.

Is it the same for you and me? Even if we do have to find out the hard way that we have wasted the resources we were going to need—and that includes invisible resources such as time, diligence, and honesty—we can repent. We can change our thinking. We can rally. With God's help, we can let our current crisis motivate us to overcome not only the bad circumstances, but also the bad habits that contributed to the crisis in the first place.

Bottom Line

To overcome a crisis—bottom line—you need to cultivate godly management skills. How can you do that? That's what this book is about.

We are the caretakers of the earth that God created, and He is our personal Caretaker as we do so.

You will learn to be a manager, a caretaker, by paying attention to your Caretaker. The more closely you walk with Him, the better. He cares so much for you that He keeps leading you into His truth. He uses every crisis situation to advance His work in your life. In His care for you, He will correct and instruct you. He will equip you so that you can please Him as you learn to manage your little corner of the planet, becoming, like Joseph, victorious over every crisis.

Chapter 3

The Management Mandate

"Your faith is only as strong as the crisis it survives."

Did you know that in the beginning, when God created the earth, He held off from sending the rain at first? He did not want to water the plants yet because He did not want them to grow before He had created someone in His own image to take care of them.

How do I know that? The second chapter of the Book of Genesis tells about it:

...When the Lord God made the earth and the heavens— and no shrub of the field had yet appeared on the earth and no plant of the field had yet sprung up, for the Lord God had not sent rain on the earth and there was no man to work the ground (Genesis 2:4-5).

God did not allow anything to grow on the earth at first because there was nobody to work the ground. The King

James Bible translates *work* as "till" the ground. Nobody had been created yet to cultivate the plants, and God did not want to let the plants grow untended.

Another way of saying it is that there was nobody to *manage* the gardening. In fact, the ancient Hebrew word that gets translated as "work" and "till" is the word `*abad,* and one of the basic meanings of this word is both "to serve" and "to cause someone or something else to serve," in other words, "to manage."

That is amazing! God did not allow anything to grow on the earth at first because He did not have a manager yet. And then He made the earth's first manager, Adam. He made Him in His own image, and He breathed His own life into him. He spoke to Adam, and Adam spoke to Him.

Now God could water the earth, causing green plants to grow in profusion. He created a wonderful garden filled with these plants and trees, and He called it Eden. He gave the Garden to Adam as his dwelling place, and He told him "to work it and take care of it" (see Gen. 2:8-15). He also told him to name the animals. And then God blessed Adam with a wife, and she was called Eve. Everything was perfect.

We Are Managers, Like Adam

Adam could not have been expected to know automatically what he was supposed to do. So God had to give him instructions. He told Adam and Eve:

"Be fruitful and increase in number; fill the earth and subdue it. Rule over the fish of the sea and the birds of the air and over every living creature that moves on the ground."

Then God said, "I give you every seed-bearing plant on the face of the whole earth and every tree that has fruit with seed in it. They will be yours for food. And to all the beasts of the earth and all the birds of the air and all the creatures that move on the ground—everything that has the breath of life in it—I give every green plant for food" (Genesis 1:28-30).

All along, God's motivation, His reason for creating the human race, was management. You could refer to these words as His "management mandate."

These words express God's original intent. They show us that His original purposes for the planet we call Earth were both simple and complicated at the same time: simple, in that He wanted to establish His Kingdom rule on earth; complicated, in that He had created such a profusion of life that managing it (as Adam found out a little later) was not going to be easy. God had given a big responsibility to a very fallible being.

When Adam and Eve rebelled against Him, He did not change the mandate. He only changed the conditions under which it would be performed. We have inherited those conditions, and we have also inherited the mandate.

Centuries and centuries later, billions of people live on the same planet called Earth. Only a fraction of them have ever known anything about God's original intention for them. Instinctively, because they have been made in His image, they know they are supposed to manage *something*. But, unaware of the One who created them and buffeted by endless challenges to their survival and happiness, most of them do not know that this impulse to be managers comes from God and that He wants them to bring His Kingdom management to the planet they live on.

They know little or nothing about the principles of the Kingdom of God. Most of them do not even realize that they are potential citizens of such a kingdom. Certainly, they have not comprehended that the Kingdom of God has a culture of its own, and laws, and a purpose for existence, just as their earthly countries and kingdoms do.

One of the psalms says, "May you be blessed by the Lord, the Maker of heaven and earth. The highest heavens belong to the Lord, but the earth He has given to man" (Ps. 115: 15-16). The Lord of Heaven and earth has given the earth into the hands of men and women. What the psalm does not say is that humankind has not done a very good job of managing that gift. In fact, people seem to have done their best to mess it up. Satan has inserted himself into the equation as well. By this time, eons after the Garden of Eden, it can be hard to tell who is most at fault.

The earth is groaning (see Rom. 8:22). The whole world lurches from one crisis to another. Ever since the Fall, the planet and its unmanageable population have been in a management crisis. Any of the individual events that we term a "crisis" stems from the underlying management crisis of the human race. God, who never gives up (and whose heavenly Kingdom, remember, is never in a crisis), has been working to regain that Kingdom-on-earth ever since, one human heart at a time.

Jesus, God's only Son, came to earth in person. His disciples asked Him how they should pray. He told them to pray like this:

> *Our Father in heaven,*
> > *may Your name be kept holy.*
>
> *May Your Kingdom come soon.*
>
> *May Your will be done on earth,*
> > *as it is in heaven* (Matthew 6:9-10 NLT).

Jesus taught them, and us, to call on His Father to restore Kingdom rule to the earth, to make it as it had been (briefly) in the Garden of Eden, when Adam and Eve were managing the newly established outpost of Heaven. In the Garden, just as in the Kingdom of Heaven, God's living Word was the law of the land. Life was good. The word *crisis* was not in their vocabulary.

To this day, as people voluntarily put themselves under His lordship, they can become citizens of the Kingdom. Over time, they can learn the culture of Heaven. They can learn God's principles, and they can learn to receive His help to obey Him. In places across the globe, they too can establish new outposts of the Kingdom. You and I can be part of this grand restoration effort.

While the word *crisis* will remain in the vocabulary of citizens of Heaven as long as they live on this troubled globe called Earth, the word will have a redemptive ring. The same "management mandate" applies to us as 21st-century citizens of the Kingdom. Our job is to follow His leading and to spread the government and culture of the Kingdom of Heaven wherever we go, until "the earth will be filled with the knowledge of the glory of the Lord, as the waters cover the sea" (Hab. 2:14).

Clashing Cultures

Managing the resources of the earth would have been a full-time job even without the Fall and everything that happened afterward. But the Fall initiated a torrent of crisis situations. From that moment on, "working the earth" would cost blood, sweat, and tears (see Gen. 3). Within a couple of decades, Abel murdered Cain (see Gen. 4).

Discord in families escalated into wars between people groups. Diseases spread. Starvation wiped out men, women, and children. All of the effects of crisis became commonplace. I listed these in the first chapter: fear, trauma, depression, despair, frustration, anxiety, loneliness, worry, hopelessness, abandonment, loss, urgency for survival, abuse, crime. We refer to these things as the "human condition." They represent a clash of the culture of God's Kingdom and its miserable imitation, the culture of humankind.

As the centuries unfolded and the human population spread across the face of the earth, the people took their sin and strife with them. When we read the historical books of the Old Testament, we are reading only a small part of the whole sorry chronicle. God's establishment of the Kingdom of Heaven on earth has been continually frustrated by the petty kingdom ambitions of human beings.

Those self-centered human ambitions have been encouraged by God's enemy, who was trying to usurp God's authority back in the Garden and who is still trying. He has made sure that the deplorable state of the world seems normal to its inhabitants. He has deceived those who were created to populate the Kingdom of Heaven on earth. Essentially, he has replaced the original heavenly culture with a cheap imitation.

In a more limited way, that is what happens whenever the culture of one nation gets imposed upon the pre-existing culture of another. During the time that the Bahamas was a colony of Great Britain, which lasted for over 200 years, we lost our distinct culture. We Bahamians used to be a wonderful blend of Caribbean and African. But 200 years is a long time. A lot of generations were born, lived, and died by the end of our years as a colony. Our old culture was buried by the new one.

For 200 years, Bahamians were British subjects, and they learned to act like British people. The government took away our language and replaced it with the "king's English." Most Bahamian people are of African descent, but none of them speak the languages of their ancestors anymore. Then the colonizers took away our African history. Instead of learning about famous African kings, we learned about King Henry

VIII and Queen Elizabeth I. The colonial governors also imposed British culture on Bahamian culture. We started drinking tea all the time. In our schools, we waved little Union Jacks as we began each day by singing "Rule Britannia." We were indoctrinated into the customs of the culture of Great Britain until the indigenous blended African and Caribbean culture all but vanished.

This same thing has happened across the globe wherever humans have settled. I am not saying that the conquering nation is always evil, but I want you to see how it works. Do you see how the devil has done the same thing to the human race?

First, he took away our language, our ability to freely communicate with our King. Then he enslaved us, and he made sure that we forgot all about our former country, which is Heaven. Next, he obliterated our memories of God's loving Fatherhood. He substituted a strange collection of false gods and began to perpetrate false beliefs all over the planet.

Last of all, he did the most damage when he made human beings forget the culture that should have been natural to them, the culture of the heavenly realm. He caused the creatures that God had created to act like *him*, the fallen angel who had become a rebel and a liar. Under his tutelage, we perfected the "art" of deception and depraved living, forgetting about the abundance of righteousness, peace, and joy that characterizes the culture of Heaven.

You and I have been born into that kind of culture clash. Nothing has improved as time has passed. Each generation thinks theirs has the worst problems. When the United

Nations was established after World War II, it was supposed to prevent further wars. Yet in only about 60 years, the world has seen more wars than in all the rest of recorded human history. In a similar way, all other well-intentioned efforts have failed. Today, the instantaneous, worldwide reporting of developing news makes us even more aware of the magnitude of upheaval everywhere.

Now we are facing a new round of crises. The people of the world are sleepless, tossing and turning with anxiety, but the people of God are going to be able to rise to the challenges before them—if they can see the difference between the worldly culture that surrounds them and the Kingdom culture that flows out from their hearts.

The people of God are the ones who have had the eyes of their hearts opened to the truth. They are required to continue to live in the midst of the man-made, satanically motivated culture of the people around them, but they have relearned the language of Heaven. They have repented of their former rebellion, and they have embraced the rule of the One who sent His Son to rescue them from slavery.

It is up to them—and now I am speaking to myself as well as to you—to shoulder once again the role that Adam and Eve forfeited when they sinned. It is up to us to endorse God's management mandate and work to restore Kingdom rule.

Management Testing

When you accept God's management mandate for yourself, you will be tested. No exceptions. Paul wrote, "...We speak as men approved by God to be entrusted with the gospel. We are not trying to please men but God, who tests our hearts" (1 Thess. 2:4). James added, "because you know that the testing of your faith develops perseverance" (James 1:3).

Where does the testing come from? Sometimes we can tell that the tests have come directly from God. Sometimes they have been caused by other people. Sometimes they seem to come straight from the evil one. Frequently, our tests come through crisis-ridden circumstances. Always, regardless of who is responsible, the tests come with the permission of God, and He stands ready to help us every minute.

Management testing comes with a price. Paying the price means passing the test. You may have to shed some of your pride. You may have to pray a heavy price of time-investment. You may lose money instead of gaining it. Sometimes the price is very high indeed. The elderly apostle John, who had suffered throughout his adult life for the Gospel, wrote a prophetic message to some of his fellow Christians from the island of Patmos, to which he had been exiled:

> *Do not be afraid of what you are about to suffer. I tell you, the devil will put some of you in prison to test you, and you will suffer persecution for ten days. Be faithful, even to the point of death, and I* [the Lord Jesus] *will give you the crown of life* (Revelation 2:10).

John himself, although he outlived the rest of the original apostles, had to pay that high price. He considered death to be the ultimate test, the culmination of many trials and long persecution.

In the previous chapter, I showed you how Joseph's management skills were tested, time and time again. He passed every test with flying colors. He paid a heavy price in the form of rejection, pain, loneliness, and homesickness. He laid down his pride (and, remember, he was quite arrogant as a teenager), his status, his career, and his inheritance. The hard blows that he suffered should have defeated him. And yet he clung to his God and to his God-given gifts and godly character traits, which only increased as he matured.

Joseph was a foreigner and a slave. He should not have been able to get out of prison. He should not have been able to rise in the ranks of governing officials as he did.

In spite of being an outsider, it was Joseph's *management* that promoted him. Pharaoh said, "Joseph, I am going to put you in charge of the whole country because you have a management plan." Joseph had proven already that he would be consistent, hard-working, honest, and forward-thinking. He proved it once again during the famine and his diligent preparations for it.

I want you to understand that it is your management that will promote you, too. If you do not already believe it, just look at what the *absence* of qualities of good management can do to your prospects for advancement.

At a management seminar, I listened to a talk by a man who operates a meat-packing plant. He described their problem with employee theft. (In the Bahamas, we call it "tiefing.") He could tell that employees were stealing a lot of the product because he could count the chickens before and after they were processed. He said, "We know we brought in three thousand chickens. At the end, we had only two thousand. What happened to a thousand of the chickens? Where were the chickens going? These chickens didn't have wings. They were dead; they couldn't fly...."

His employees did not have wings to fly with, either, but they did have feet to walk with—along with their "sticky fingers" to steal with. I would be very surprised if any of those employees ever get a raise or get promoted, and I would not be shocked to hear that some of them had been fired. What if the head of the meat-packing plant could bring in a "Joseph" to supervise the operation? I think that things would improve. He would break up their racket!

He would break through their sense of entitlement, which is a particular problem in the Bahamas, but also in many other places. "Why shouldn't I help myself?" they say to themselves, "They ain't paying me enough anyway, so I'm carrying some of this chicken." Does this sound familiar?

That's justifying evil. God is taking notes. He is looking for honesty and diligence. He rewards the person who works hard and who manages his affairs with integrity. He allows a crisis of conscience in order to test the quality of your character. Do you have the character of a good manager?

Have you been passing your management tests? Have you been tempted to rely on your own strength because you were desperate (or merely because of that sense of entitlement)? If you have fallen to some kind of temptation, it is not too late to start building a better personal history. Repent and start with a clean slate. Start living by Kingdom principles.

You will find more blessings that way than you will by living by your self-centered human insight.

Go to work tomorrow and clean up around your desk or wherever you work. Make excellence your goal. Don't shirk your duties. Work as if God is watching you—because He is.

Then when you go home, do the same thing. Even if you are renting an apartment in a bad neighborhood, keep that place up to the best of your ability. Keep the windows just as clean as you keep your soul.

I am sure that even when Joseph was living in that dirty prison, he did his best to pull his hair out of his eyes and to keep his prison-issue loincloth clean. God was watching Joseph in prison, even when his family and the pharaoh could not see him. God was watching to see if Joseph would pass this test the same way he had passed his other tests. How would he manage his very limited resources in that prison? Would he lie or steal? Would he become fearful or angry? Would he withdraw into a sullen depression?

Because Joseph passed the test, he was promoted. In his new role, he had more honor, but he also had more responsibility. He attained greater wealth, and he had more authority, but he had to work even harder and call on the name of the Lord even more.

God can use a man or woman like that to help establish His Kingdom in the midst of the "prison" of any kingdom on earth.

Effective Management Determines Your Resources

Joseph's story shows us how effective management determines what resources will be available to a person. More than once, Joseph's crisis was that he was reduced to nothing. Each time, he managed himself and his almost-unmanageable circumstances so effectively that he was promoted anew.

Although it may take a long time to get there, the end result of good management is increased wealth, whether the riches are in the form of money or of things you cannot hold in your hand, such as happiness or gratification.

Jesus told an unusual story about management. Luke put it in his Gospel (see Luke 16). It is the parable about the smart manager who happened to be dishonest but who really had the makeup of an excellent manager.

Jesus commended him because of what he did after he was fired. He was fired for wasting his master's property and for lying about it. He was stunned for a minute when his master told him to leave, but the manager was a very shrewd man. He knew that he could not find another job easily. So without losing a minute, he went out and found his master's debtors. He sat down with each of them, and he renegotiated the amount of money that was outstanding on their bills. This ingratiated him to these debtors, who were rich people, and it probably guaranteed him future employment with one of them.

I sincerely doubt that his old master would have re-hired him because those new deals would have made the old master lose even more money, but Jesus says that the master *com-mended* his former manager: "The master commended the dishonest manager because he had acted shrewdly. For the people of this world are more shrewd in dealing with their own kind than are the people of the light" (Luke 16:8).

Jesus went on to make a very important point:

Whoever can be trusted with very little can also be trusted with much, and whoever is dishonest with very little will also be dishonest with much. So if you have not been trustworthy in handling worldly wealth, who will trust you with true riches? And if you have not been trustworthy with someone else's property, who will give you property of your own? (Luke 16:10-12)

God will not hand you a paycheck just for getting saved. He will only give you an income because you can manage it. He will allow your management skills—which grow alongside your godly character and your obedience—to earn you favor. The more effective your management is, the more likely it is that you will be promoted to greater responsibility and also blessed with greater resources.

Remember the chickens, remember the paper clip, and remember the shrewd manager in Jesus' story. If you are dishonest with a little, you will be dishonest with much, so you are not to be trusted as a manager. If you mismanage little things, you will mismanage big things. Then how will you get true riches?

You have to earn property rights. That is how it works. That is why most people start out their married life in a rented apartment or house. That is why most businesses and churches start out in rented facilities. You can move up after you have earned some more money, it is true, but you will be able to move up more quickly if you have earned respect for how you treated the property that you rented. God will reward you for managing your rented apartment well.

In most cities in the Western world, the people who end up renting all their lives are most often the same ones who disrespect the property-owner by disregarding the upkeep of the place. Their child breaks a tile in the bathroom? Who cares? It's just a rental property. The lightbulb burns out? Demand a new one from the landlord. Don't spend an extra dollar if you can find some way around it.

God is watching to see how well you manage what He has given you already before He will give you additional resources to manage. It will not matter to Him if you go to church three times a week and carry a Bible in every pocket. If you are not managing the situation He has set you in, He will not answer your earnest prayer for "more, more, more." (Can you imagine asking God for a million dollars? A million dollars would be too much for 90 percent of us. We'd hop on the next plane, take a luxury vacation, buy some fancy car, etc., etc. Before long, we would be broke, worse off than before.)

Last but not least, tithing is part of effective management. Tithing is God's management training program. God will watch how you manage resources by how you manage His tithe. Not that He needs the money. It is all His anyway. He is looking to see if you will be able to put aside that little 10 percent of His money.

Tithing requires accountability. It requires discipline. It requires honesty. It requires diligence, faithfulness, and trustworthiness. All of these are aspects of good management as well.

Remember what God said to the people of Israel through the prophet Malachi? He said, "You people are robbing Me." (See Malachi 3:8a.)

The people said, "How are we stealing from You?"

And He said, "In tithes and offerings" (Mal. 3:8b). He told them, "You are eating My tithe." And He made them a deal: "If you will be faithful and start paying your tithes again, then I will open the windows of Heaven, and I will pour out on you a blessing so great that you cannot contain it" (see Mal. 3:10).

That is the best example of what I mean when I say effective management determines your resources!

Adding Value

Remember my definition of management from Chapter 2: management is the effective, efficient, correct, and timely use of another person's property and resources for the purpose for which they were delegated with a view to producing the expected added value.

Have you been adding value to whatever you are doing? What does it mean to add value to what you are managing?

Are you an employee? Do not just show up at your job so you can collect a paycheck. What aspect of your employer's business do you manage? Figure out what you manage and work to improve it. Even if you are the receptionist, you can add value to your position by being alert, friendly, reliable, and hospitable, and by doing the little extra things that do not appear on your job description. Even if you are a night-shift janitor, working behind the scenes where nobody sees you, you can add value to your work by means of your diligence. Don't always look for the easy way out; instead, seek out ways to serve the people who have employed you. Go above and beyond the call of duty.

Regardless of your position, you can come up with ideas to make your employer's business grow. You can come up with strategies to make your department expand. You can think of some creative ideas to bring in more business.

Do you manage the work of other people? Build them up. Help them to do their very best. Think of ways to help them do their jobs more efficiently and smoothly. Do people make appointments with you to consult you? Serve each one of them with equal attention. Give them good legal advice or medical care or whatever you dispense. Give them more than they expected to receive. Be pleasant. Be generous with your time while at the same time being efficient, because if you get behind in your appointments, you are not adding value to the people you kept too long in your waiting room.

Do you have a family? Do not let your employment rob your family of your presence. Be there for your children. Do not take your family for granted. Let them know that you are glad they live with you. Tell them that you appreciate them. Show affection to your spouse; try to avoid being unpleasant or demanding.

Do you remember the story in the Bible about the servants who were given the talents? (See Matthew 25:14-30.) The ones who got the praise (and cash back!) were the ones who added value to the money they were given. The guy who buried his one talent in the backyard got scolded, and he got his one talent taken away too. He did not add any value to it at all. In fact, when he turned it over, it was covered with dirt.

The master used some strong language with that guy. He called him "wicked and lazy": "You wicked, lazy servant!...You should have put my money on deposit with the bankers, so that when I returned I would have received it back with interest" (Matt. 25:26-27). To God, wickedness is when you mismanage any of His resources. Wickedness is when you take something that He gave you and make it lose value. You don't ever want God to call you "wicked and lazy."

Do everything you can to pass your daily tests. Add value to your use of time. Manage it well; don't waste it. Show up on time, and leave on time. Add value to your "in-between" times; ask the Lord if you could be praying for something when you are in transit or just waiting for the next thing to happen. Add value to your relationships. Use basic good manners. Show honor and respect to other people. Think about the other person before you think about yourself. Find ways to make their day more successful.

Take a good long look at your daily routine. How can you manage it better? How can you add value to each aspect of it?

Diligence and Patience

Proverbs 10:4 says, "Lazy hands make a man poor, but diligent hands bring wealth." The opposites of laziness and poverty are *diligence* and *wealth*. Would you rather be stuck in poverty or well provided for? That's a rhetorical question; I know how you will answer.

When you meet a diligent person, you are going to meet a patient person. The two character traits go together. They help define each other. A diligent person must work long and hard. He must not give up when he is tired or discouraged. He does not demand to be entertained while he is working. He toils patiently. Likewise, a patient person must be willing to wait for results. Patience is not a passive thing. It is active because it involves doing something—*putting* your hope and trust in a certain outcome.

A patient and diligent person is a good manager. He or she is willing to keep driving the same old, beat-up car for several more years while working diligently (managing resources) to save up enough to get a new one. A patient, diligent person does not jump the gun. Why take out a loan to buy a new car when you can still drive the old one to work every day? Why pay interest on the price of the car when you do not have to? That diminishes the "added value" of your assets. It feeds your sense of entitlement and pride.

You may need to ask for help to conquer your lazy habits. You may not realize how ingrained they are, and you may need a boost from another person before you can exert the extra energy required to become a diligent manager.

Even if you seem to be a born manager, you will need to exercise your gifts and wisdom. You cannot put your life on cruise control. Keep God in the driver's seat. Let Him help you use your gifts. You will need to define your goals and your strategies, too. Here is a personal example:

When my wife and I were first married, we could not afford to buy a home. I finished my schooling and brought my wife and first child to live with my mother-in-law because we could not afford to pay rent. For four years we lived there. We drove an old red Datsun with a taped-up bumper. It was not out of laziness that we were so poor; we were just starting out as a family, and we had not yet had time to accumulate anything. That four years seemed like forever. With diligence and patience, I had to swallow my pride and keep working toward my goal.

I did have a definite goal: I wanted to save up enough to buy a house in a place called Westwood Villas. I had no intention of taking advantage of the hospitality of my wonderful mother-in-law indefinitely. When I got tired of the living arrangement, I would remind myself of the truth. Then I would go out and put another strip of duct tape on the bumper of the car. That thing would smoke as we drove down the street. No one could have accused us of living above our means.

Eventually, we got the house in Westwood Villas. Now it is paid for, and so are the three cars we have in the driveway. Since we bought the house, the property assessment amount has risen greatly, which has added value to our original investment. It was worth the price we paid, not only in money, but in diligence and patience.

The Book of Proverbs is packed full of advice about diligence. Proverbs 13:4 says, "The sluggard craves and gets nothing, but the desires of the diligent are fully satisfied." Sluggards are lazy fellows. They are always wanting to hit the jackpot, but it never seems to occur. They look outside at the sunshine and say, "Today is going to be my lucky day." They always say that they have a "plan," but they are always broke. On the opposite side, the diligent person does not give a single thought to hitting the jackpot. He does not rely on mere luck. He gets out of bed in the morning, and, without wasting time, he gets straight to work, trusting in God's strength to keep him on a straight path. His plan is a sound one because he remembers that he is a steward of God's resources.

He is the one who will succeed in the end. He will be able to overcome every setback and get back on both feet, stronger than before. It is true—"The plans of the diligent lead to profit as surely as haste leads to poverty" (Prov. 21:5).

CHAPTER 4

Seven Ways to Manage a Crisis

*Character is not made in a crisis—it is only
exhibited.* —*Robert Freeman*

When a crisis hits you, it is too late to wonder if you are ready or not. You will soon find out. And yet, regardless of whether or not you turn out to be prepared for going through a difficult time, the crisis will teach you new things.

If you have been growing and maturing as a citizen of the Kingdom of God for a while, you may be pleasantly surprised. Of course, the crisis itself will not be pleasant. But your Kingdom-style reactions to it may demonstrate that you have been learning your management lessons well. You may discover that, instead of fear and panic, you have peace in your heart. Instead of gasping for breath and grasping at straws, you may find that you are able trust God utterly, just as you have always wanted to be able to do. You may have moments of meltdown, but for the most part, you will react in a clear-headed and clear-hearted way, and you will be able to help your family and friends to do the same.

If this is you, the crisis situation will give you a review lesson. Your priorities will be put under a microscope. Have you been managing your affairs well but placing a little too much of your security in your income level? Now is the time to repent of trusting in money and realign yourself with your God, who is your Provider. Have you been faithfully attending church and tithing, but putting more trust in your pastor or in the institution of the church than in God Himself? Your crisis situation will expose the foundations under your feet. God will use it to help you grow.

If, on the other hand, you have been lax in your walk with the Lord, taking Him for granted and just living a life that looks more or less like the lives of the people around you, a crisis will wake you up with a bang. God wants to get your attention. He cares about you too much to allow you to waste your life. He wants to give you a crash course in management skills and a review of the lessons you have learned up to this point.

The very nature of a crisis will force you to learn things the hard way. You will wish that somebody would come and tell you what steps to take because your brain won't be working too well, especially when you get caught up in fear or anger.

For that reason, I want to lay out seven ways to begin to manage a crisis, especially a crisis that has financial ramifications such as a job loss, unexpectedly high bills, a family health crisis, a natural disaster, foreclosure on your home (even if you are renting your home, your landlord can suffer a foreclosure), or a national financial breakdown that affects the welfare of everyone.

In the rest of this chapter, I will explore each one of these ideas in a little more detail. How can you begin to manage a crisis? Start by evaluating your life and by doing the following:

1. Determine your needs.
2. Acquire only what you need.
3. Do not live beyond your ability.
4. Withdraw the unnecessary.
5. Delay major projects.
6. Value your possessions.
7. Save, conserve, and protect your resources.

Determine Your Needs

First, you must determine your needs. Many of us make a shopping list before we go to the store. But how many of us make lists of the true needs in our lives?

We must be clear on the difference between our needs and our "wants." When we are in a crisis, we must know the sometimes-fine distinction between our needs and our wants, and we must be able to figure it out quickly.

Most of us jumble our needs together with our "wants." We find it hard to tell the difference between them. Sometimes we just want something so badly. But wanting something very, very much will not convert it into a needful thing.

Do you really *need* that new dress you saw in the shop window? You know you don't.

Sometimes we put things into a "need" category because of what other people might say. We think we need to look the part to belong to whatever group we think we should fit in with. "What will people think if I don't even have a [fill in the blank]?" "What will people think of me now that I am divorced?" "Won't they reject me if I set up my business/church/home in that neighborhood that has a bad reputation?"

Often, we feel obligated to carry out other people's expectations. For example, perhaps you have always given expensive gadgets as Christmas gifts to your family members, but your husband has lost his job, and you have had a large number of extra expenses this past year. This Christmas, take stock of your budget, and determine to buy practical things for your family members. Keep it simple. You may even decide to make the gifts yourself. Get creative. Bake somebody a cake, and put his name on it. Grow some flowers in pretty pots. Offer to give your time and skill to help people with projects around their houses. You do not have to let your former lavish gift-giving dictate what you do this year.

In a crisis, your wants must go away. This is not the time to fret about that beautiful something-or-other that you had your eye on. You may be used to eating out for lunch every day. This is the time to start carrying your lunch from home. Don't whine, "But I still want to go out to a meal with my friends at least once a week." You may want to do that, but now it is crisis time, and you need to stay home and cook.

Resolve today to figure out the difference between your true needs and your wants. God does not want you to live in a gray zone. Indecision and fuzzy thinking will put you in a dangerous position: the middle of the road. You do not want to live there. If you are out there in the middle of the road, one crisis after another will keep running you over.

Acquire Only What You Need

What once seemed like a good idea—purchasing that nice piece of property on the other side of town—will not look like such a smart plan when your income is in jeopardy. When a crisis hits, all of a sudden you do not need that piece of property anymore. If you go and buy it anyway, you may regret it. You may end up with a worthless piece of land.

In a crisis, as far as your acquisitions are concerned, push the "pause" button. Buy only what you are reasonably sure you will need. If you know a hurricane is coming, go and buy some jugs of bottled water and a couple of flashlight batteries, but skip the sale on lawn furniture. If you have made an adequate determination of the difference between your needs and your wants, it will not be so difficult to put a limit on what you acquire. Acquire only what you need.

In a crisis situation, you are going to need liquid assets. You are going to need money to spend on necessary purchases and to settle outstanding debts. The currency in your wallet and the coins in your pocket are liquid assets. The money in your bank accounts such as savings and checking accounts is a liquid asset because you can gain access to it quickly.

In a crisis situation, you do not need more fixed assets, such as the piece of property I mentioned above. Your home, even if it is worth a lot of money, is a fixed asset. Selling it and converting its value into cash will take a long time, and in a time of regional crisis, that transaction may be unachievable.

Do Not Live Beyond Your Means

In a time of crisis—or any time, for that matter—you should not live beyond your ability to pay your bills and to maintain what you have acquired. This is simple common sense. Too often, however, it seems that simple common sense is a rare commodity. It is a matter of needs versus wants again.

Check your bank account. Take a look into your wallet. Add up those bills. Is your income ahead of your spending? Or is your spending ahead of your income? Are you using credit too much?

Living within your means—what a foreign concept to some of us! We operate out of skewed thinking. To be honest, we are "living within our wants" most of the time. And we wonder why we are in trouble. As the months go by, we become magnets for crisis, and our personal crisis cannot be blamed on anybody but ourselves.

Live within your means. Make a *decision* to do so. Tell somebody else about it. Become accountable to follow through on what you have decided. Ask for advice if you need to. Far better to lose a little pride than to lose your shirt.

Withdraw From the Unnecessary

When you have determined the difference between your true needs and your "extras," you can draw the line between the necessaries and the *un*necessaries. The necessaries of life are the things you truly need—food, shelter, and a little bit more. The unnecessaries include the luxuries—that club membership, that shopping expedition, those tickets to the concert series.

Yes, you will have to sacrifice. Someday you may be able to have it again, but not right now. Remember, everything you "own" is not yours anyway. It belongs to God, and you are the steward of it. When times are tough, far be it from you to act as if you are wiser than God, who reminds you that you were bought with a price, and you are not your own (see 1 Cor. 6:19-20). As the New Living Translation puts it, "…You do not belong to yourself, for God bought you with a high price…."

If you revise your spending habits, you may have a surplus, which you can give away to other people. We tend to forget about the importance of being able to give to other people. If you are squandering your time and your money on unnecessary things, you will not have anything left over to give away. "…God loves a cheerful giver" (2 Cor. 9:7), and "whoever sows sparingly will also reap sparingly, and whoever sows generously will also reap generously" (2 Cor. 9:6). When you are so busy running around spending money, you may not even have any *time* to give to others. It will be hard to justify your extra spending when you are driving your SUV to the gym and you approach that intersection where you always see the guy with the cardboard sign on which he has scrawled, "Will work for food."

Withdraw from the unnecessary. Your life should not consist of running around spending money. It is OK to withdraw from expensive obligations, especially in a time of crisis.

It is also OK to withdraw from certain friendships if they are dragging you down. You may think that it does not matter what kind of people you associate with, but it does. Jesus said, "Can a blind man lead a blind man? Will they not both fall into a pit?" (Luke 6:39). Some people get stuck in crisis mode because they are afraid of conflict and they cannot disassociate from friends who are spiritually blind.

Disassociation does not have to be confrontational. You can ease out of people's lives quietly and keep your integrity in the process. When they notice that they haven't seen you in a while, you can just smile and say, "Well, I've been real busy." When a whole year goes by and you have not stopped to say "Hi," you can admit that you have been working on some projects, doing some extra things, fulfilling some responsibilities. You can be like Nehemiah, who responded to the people who wanted to distract him from rebuilding the walls of Jerusalem: "I am carrying on a great project and cannot go down. Why should the work stop while I leave it and go down to you?" (Neh. 6:3).

Delay Major Projects

While you should remain busy and work hard, you should not undertake big, new projects in a time of crisis. This is another variation on the same idea: in a time of crisis, make a conscious decision to curtail your plans for improving your property or whatever you manage. Governments are doing it. Companies are doing it. You have to do it, too.

When a major company cuts back, the people in upper management do not seem to have any feelings. They say things like, "Cut the staff 35 percent," and then they walk out of the boardroom. They don't care who has to go. They don't care how you did it. They don't care if they hired some of those staff members personally. Just "cut the staff 35 percent," and that is *it*. That is how you have to be in your personal life right now, because in a crisis, you can't hesitate because of your feelings.

Did you think this would be the year to install that new air conditioning system? Put that on hold, and get the old one fixed. The market is doing crazy things, and you cannot be sure that you will be able to pay the price of a new system. If you have reservations, do not take the risk.

Regroup and try again later after the tide of the crisis has ebbed.

Value Your Possessions

I like this suggestion most of all. It stimulates resourcefulness, and at the same time it cultivates an "attitude of gratitude."

Whether your possessions are few or you have more possessions than you can count, take stock of them with fresh eyes. They are valuable. Thank God for each item, big or small. Look for the unusual things—that little pot you keep your house key in, the wooden table next to the front door where you put the pot, the house key itself.

Thank the Lord for His provision for you. Thank Him for whatever occurs to you, such as the family member who gave you that pot, or for the roof over your head that the key represents. Just appreciate the gifts and resources that you otherwise take for granted. It will be good for your soul. This simple exercise of gratitude can keep you from suffering from the disease of dissatisfaction, which often drives people to say, "I want more! Give me more, more, more!"

Next consider how to better use the things you are now grateful for. Do you have a big house, with only one person (you) living in it? Could you rent out some of the extra bedrooms? Could you contribute some of the furniture to a single mother who has none? Would it make sense to set up your office space at home? In a way, those extra rooms are dead. You are only one person; you don't need four bedrooms to sleep in.

Making better use of your possessions is good management. You are adding value to something that was just sitting there gathering dust.

What do you have outside your house? Do you keep two cars, even though you can only use one of them at a time? Why keep wasting your time and money maintaining two cars? This could be a good time to try to sell one of them. Turn that possession into liquid cash, and put it in the bank. Give or sell it to your nephew for a price he can afford, so he can have a vehicle to commute to college.

What about that big truck you bought awhile ago? Could you turn that truck into something? Maybe it could become a weekend business for you. You could use it to move things for people who don't have a truck. Do you see what I mean?

Value everything you possess. Especially in a time of financial crisis, you never know how useful your possessions may prove to be.

Save, Conserve, and Protect Your Resources

I meet people all the time who seem to think that "save" is a four-letter word, in a negative sense. They just cannot do it, or so they say. After we sit down and talk for a while, they begin to see that if they change their spending habits and protect their assets, they can save after all. Sometimes I send them to financial advisors who can provide some wisdom for them. They need structure. They need a plan. They need to be decisive rather than impulsive about what they do with their money.

Save, conserve, and protect are very similar terms. If you had a chalkboard or a whiteboard in front of you and I told you to draw three pictures to illustrate "Save," "Conserve," and "Protect," chances are good that your three pictures would look similar. I would draw a big heap of items, and put a fence around it. If I asked you to demonstrate with your bare hands what these three words mean, you might make gathering-in motions and then covering-up motions, like a mother hen protecting her chicks under her wings.

Bahamians have a notoriously difficult time saving, conserving, and protecting. So do Americans. The Commerce Department of the United States government has a division that is called the Bureau of Economic Analysis. The BEA puts out a quarterly report of the rate at which American citizens save their money in the bank. From the beginning of 2005 through 2006, 2007, and the first part of 2008, the savings rate was less than 1 percent in almost every quarter. In one quarter of 2005, it dipped below the zero line, which had not happened since the 1930s during the Great Depression.

The savings rate crept up slightly as the economic crisis intensified in 2008, but it remains very low. People are still living paycheck to paycheck, depending on credit cards, and hoping that they will not lose their jobs. As unemployment rates soar, more and more people will discover that they should have been "saving for a rainy day."

They need new habits of taking care of what they have already, and I am not talking only about money. Our possessions are also our resources. As I have been saying throughout this book, it is important to learn to use the things that you already own. Don't just toss them out and buy new ones. The early settlers had the right idea when they used everything up, fixed whatever got broken, and re-used things after they were no longer useful for their original purposes.

If you are short of money, you don't need a handout or a windfall from the lottery. You need management. You need to learn to steward your resources with God's wisdom. You need to save, conserve, and protect the provision He gives you.

Seek First the Kingdom

As you are saving, conserving, and protecting your resources, you do not need to hoard your money or your possessions. You are a Kingdom citizen, and the King wants you to trust Him. You do not have to be anxious about saving enough just as you do not have to worry about becoming a good manager of the resources He has given you to take care of. He will help you.

Many of us have a false view of prosperity. For starters, we think it means excess. We ignore the Bible verses that warn us about the dangers of prosperity. (We must think those verses could not possibly apply to us because even the truly rich want more and do not feel as prosperous as they think they should.) The Bible reports that the people who are burdened with excess wealth have to spend all of their time and energy protecting it. And for what purpose? As long as it is being hoarded, it is not doing anybody any good. Too much money can give you headaches and make you depressed. You put bars on the windows and deadbolts on the doors, worrying all night that someone might steal your wealth.

Remember the story of the wealthy farmer in Luke 12 and the warnings in the fifth chapter of James.

Now listen, you rich people, weep and wail....Your wealth has rotted, and moths have eaten your clothes. Your gold and silver are corroded....You have hoarded wealth in the last days....You have lived on earth in luxury and self-indulgence. You have fattened yourselves in the day of slaughter (James 5:1-3, 5).

After telling the story of the wealthy farmer who died before he could enjoy his riches, and after talking about how the Lord provides for the birds of the air and the lilies of the field, Jesus said this:

Do not set your heart on what you will eat or drink; do not worry about it. For the pagan world runs after all such things, and your Father knows that you need them. But seek His kingdom, and these things will be given to you as well.

Do not be afraid, little flock, for your Father has been pleased to give you the kingdom. Sell your possessions and give to the poor. Provide purses for yourselves that will not wear out, a treasure in heaven that will not be exhausted, where no thief comes near and no moth destroys. For where your treasure is, there your heart will be also (Luke 12:29-34).

In the end, it is all about the Kingdom. Whether you live in poverty or in wealth, whether you suffer the effects of war or enjoy a time of unbroken peace, God wants you to be contented in your spirit (see Phil. 4:11). He wants you to take practical measures to overcome every crisis and sometimes to head them off before they have a chance to hit. But most of all He wants you to live as a trustful, relaxed citizen of the Kingdom of Heaven. Even when you are working 16 hours a day and sweating buckets, you can have a peaceful spirit. That's the best way to live.

Living by Faith

We live in a consumer-driven culture, and it is in a crisis all the time. The society around us is obsessed with *things*. People are perpetually tired and worn out, distracted and depressed, irritable and in a hurry. They suffer from stress-induced illnesses, and they treat each other poorly.

The Kingdom of God is not like that in the least. The resources we need are supposed to come to us in the natural course of living our lives according to God's design and intention. We do not seek the Kingdom of God because of its benefits, but its benefits come to us as we seek the Kingdom. The provisions and resources that we need are not meant to become the objects of our faith. They are meant to be the by-products of our faith.

Kingdom-dwellers have faith. Their faith grows as they exercise it daily. True Kingdom people do not treat their faith as a tool or a trick. When they exercise their faith, it is not like playing a slot machine, where if they somehow end up with the right combination of words and actions, they win.

Rather, it is a relationship, albeit with an invisible King. This King of ours has communicated liberally with His people, especially through His written Word. He has displayed his laws and His principles and has made them accessible to all who have eyes to see and ears to hear.

God's Son, Jesus, came to preach the Kingdom of God. He did not confuse His listeners when He said, "Seek first the kingdom of God and His righteousness, and all these things shall be added to you" (Matt. 6:33 NKJV). For a member of the family of the Kingdom, what was truly worth seeking? Only two things: the Kingdom itself and the righteousness that comes from God.

A Kingdom person does not live for a job. A Kingdom person does not live for a spouse. A Kingdom person does not live to gather blessings. Rather a Kingdom person lives to display the love of God to the society around him or her. A Kingdom person may revert to old habits of self-protection, but soon remembers that God wants to supply every need.

The King is both Father and Savior. He is omnipotent, which means "all-powerful." He is omniscient, which means "all-knowing." He is omnipresent, which means He is everywhere at the same time.

Therefore, we can say with Paul, who wrote to the Roman Christians in their ongoing crisis situations:

> *Who shall separate us from the love of Christ? Shall trouble or hardship or persecution or famine or nakedness or danger or sword?* [In other words, every crisis known to the world.] *As it is written:*
>
> *"For your sake we face death all day long;*
> *we are considered as sheep to be slaughtered."*
>
> *No, in all these things we are more than conquerors through Him who loved us.* [We are overcomers.] *For I am con-*

vinced that neither death nor life, neither angels nor demons, neither the present nor the future, nor any powers, neither height nor depth, nor anything else in all creation, will be able to separate us from the [unconquerable, ever-present] *love of God that is in Christ Jesus our Lord* (Romans 8:35-39).

Pay attention to the notes I added to these verses. For Kingdom people, these verses are important words. They express the message of this book—that there is no crisis too big for God. He will make sure that His people can conquer and overcome anything because His love is never overshadowed by any crisis.

CHAPTER 5

Overcoming Seasons of Crisis

Crises and deadlocks when they occur have at least this advantage, that they force us to think.
—*Jawaharlal Nehru*

Everything is seasonal. No matter where you live, the seasons come and go—summer, autumn, winter, and spring. In different regions of the world, those seasons look quite different, but each season always has some positive aspects and some negative aspects. The view from your window may be green or brown or white. The temperature may be hot or cold. The weather may be cloudy and rainy or clear and dry. To a large extent, those are seasonal differences.

People are always looking forward with expectation to the next season or the next one after that, and they are glad when they get there. Farmers, fishermen, and other people who work outdoors probably have the best appreciation for the reality of seasonal change, but all of us are completely familiar with seasonal patterns.

Human life seems to be seasonal as well. Looking at the broad scope, we observe that birth and infancy are like the seedtime and new growth of spring. We talk about youth and young adulthood as being like a long fruitful summer season. Middle age is compared to autumn, when everything is ripe for harvest and summer's growth begins to slow down. Old age is very much like winter, but even in winter there is beauty and hard-won wisdom—and the very real hope of new life.

In the ups and downs of our individual lives, we see that each of our years has seasons too. Seasons of busy activity give way to seasons of rest. Seasons of serenity alternate with seasons of trouble. Seasons of calm are shattered by seasons of crisis. Sometimes we move from one season to another fairly quickly, but other times it seems to happen with agonizing slowness.

Within each life, there is an ebb and flow that is as certain as the tide, whether the person's life has very little trouble in it or whether the person seems to barely survive one calamity after another. Our lives move in and out. And just as nobody on the face of the earth is immune from crisis, so also nobody suffers in high crisis mode forever.

Always Turning

Some people do not like change. But even those people realize that seasonal change has many benefits. They understand that the earth needs a rest between growing seasons. It needs to gather nutrients and become ready for the coming growing season. They understand that times of plenty, while they may be followed by times of lack, will be followed again in due time by more seasons of plenty. They appreciate the different kinds of beauty that accompany each of the seasons.

God is the one who established the seasons of the year. He is the one who created climate differences. He made the tropics, and He made Antarctica. He made the oceans, and He made the mountains. He is the founding Father of seasonal change.

In the Book of Ecclesiastes, we read this familiar statement. You can replace the word *time* with the word *season* throughout:

> *There is a time for everything,*
> > *and a season for every activity under heaven:*
>
> *a time to be born and a time to die,*
> > *a time to plant and a time to uproot,*
>
> *a time to kill and a time to heal,*
> > *a time to tear down and a time to build,*
>
> *a time to weep and a time to laugh,*
> > *a time to mourn and a time to dance,*
>
> *a time to scatter stones and a time to gather them,*
> > *a time to embrace and a time to refrain,*
>
> *a time to search and a time to give up,*
> > *a time to keep and a time to throw away,*
>
> *a time to tear and a time to mend,*
> > *a time to be silent and a time to speak,*

a time to love and a time to hate,
　　a time for war and a time for peace
(Ecclesiastes 3:1-8).

Did you notice how many of those times are times of crisis? Dying, uprooting, killing, tearing down, "scattering stones," weeping, mourning, searching, throwing away, tearing, hating, warring....

Yet every time of crisis is balanced out by a time of joy: birthing, planting, healing, building, laughing, dancing, gathering, embracing, finding, keeping, mending, reconciliation, love, joy, peace....

Yes, everything is seasonal. Everything changes. Before long, even if you are now in a difficult season, a new season will appear.

Nothing Is Permanent—Except God

Another way of putting it is this: "Nothing is permanent." Although the seasonal cycles can become predictable, they do keep changing.

I should modify that statement to say that nothing is permanent *except God and His promises.* The leaves may fall from the trees, and the weather may change, but God never changes. He is the same yesterday, today, and forever (see Heb. 13:8).

God, the Unchanging One, is the One who set up the ever-changing seasons of the earth and of our lives. And He knew what He was doing. For one thing, He wanted His people to understand that they do not need to worry about their lives. Whatever is happening is not permanent. God is in charge of all of the changes. Therefore, it does not matter what is happening because it cannot last. There will be an end to every crisis.

It does not matter if what is happening seems good to you or if it seems bad because it will change eventually, and your God orchestrates the changing. Seasons are His way of guaranteeing improvement. This means that seasonal change is one of His most consistent ways of bringing *hope*. This means that you do not throw your hope away, even in the darkest season of your life. After all, no matter how cold you get in the winter, you always know summer is coming. Likewise, when winter comes, you do not throw away your swim trunks. You know the summer will come around again. You know you will need those swim trunks—but when you jump in the water to go swimming, you will not need the long-sleeved pullover you may have been wearing in the middle of the winter.

In the same way, when a "wintery" economic season comes upon you, do not throw away your bank account, even if it seems useless. Leave some money in it to keep it open. Why? Because the season is coming when you will be able to add more money to it again. Everything is seasonal, times of plenty and times of poverty. Winter never stays. Summer never stays, either.

Both employment and unemployment are seasonal. If you are unemployed, then a time of employment lies ahead. If this is the season for you to leave your job, then a better job is up ahead. You have got to close out one chapter in order to open up the next one. Most of the time, you have to get ready for a chapter that is bigger and better than the one before.

To everything there is a season. Times of crisis are temporary. This is good.

The Key to Life Is Outlasting the Season

If you are in a season of crisis, waiting for the season to change can be challenging. You need more than patient endurance. You need true hope. If you know that there is a light at the end of the tunnel and if you can keep God at your side helping you, you can outlast the darkest season.

If you can stay warm and hold out through the long, cold winter, you will make it to summer. It is a sure thing. As long as you can keep holding out your hands to the fire of God's Kingdom presence, even if your body remains chilled and shivering, you can endure until the shivering stops and the sun shines again.

Your life is a walk of faith. And as I reminded you in Chapter 1, in the words of the apostle John: "Everyone born of God overcomes the world. This is the victory that has overcome the world, even our faith" (1 John 5:4). Your *faith* is what keeps you going through the low times. Your faith informs your decisions and fuels your determination.

When John says that your faith overcomes the "world," he is using the word *cosmos* in Greek. That means the governing systems, the systems of influence, the patterns of personal power and dominance. In other words, you can overcome the cosmos—the economies and cultures of the world. You may have to suffer trials for a season, but in the long run, you can overcome the system that is so broken.

Yes, the system is broken. Banks are collapsing, insurance companies are folding up, oil prices are fluctuating, businesses are downsizing, the economy is going belly up. But you can watch it all go by, confident that God will show you the next step. You can outlast this discouraging season, too, just as you outlasted the previous ones.

We tend to panic too quickly. We throw up our hands in despair rather than reaching up our hands to God. We need to "stand still, and see the salvation of the Lord" (Exod. 14:13 NKJV). We need to outlast the threats and dangers of the season of crisis. The Lord Himself will bring us into the next season, a season of safety. You cannot see the salvation of the Lord unless you stand steady. Do not run the other way, because He has you in the right position. Right here is where you will see and receive your salvation from this predicament, just as the people of Israel saw the Red Sea open up, delivering them from the spears and chariots of the advancing Egyptian army.

Seasons Give the Incentive to Plan for the Future

During a season of crisis, we would do well to exercise our faith by planning for the future season that we believe is coming. When God saves us—not *from* the storm but rather *through* the storm—we gain the incentive to go forward into the future. Knowing that this season will not last, we can prepare for the one that is coming.

You know, the best time to buy holiday supplies is a year in advance, when they are on sale right after the holiday is over. By the same token, the best time to shop for winter clothes can be in the hot summer, when nobody else wants them.

So in your season of drought, clean out your cisterns in advance preparation for a well-watered season. In your season of prosperity, save up for your next season of shortage. The seasons are always moving.

Put your hope in God. You know why they call Him the Rock of Ages—because the ages keep passing Him by. The age of brokenness passes Him by. The age of plenty passes too. The age of submission passes by. The age of confusion passes. Whatever kind of crisis, that age or season passes by too, and the Rock is steady.

With Him and in His circle of protection, you and I are durable. Plant your feet on the Rock and look toward the bright horizon of your future.

Never Respond Permanently to a Temporary Problem

Do not throw your hands up and say, "That's it! It's over. I am not going to make it." If you do that, you are trying to make a permanent condition out of a temporary experience. What causes you to think that this current season of crisis will never end? It *will* end. It is temporary.

Do not give up the ship just because a storm hits. Do not throw away your winter clothes just because summer has arrived. Those are permanent solutions to temporary problems. This season will change into the next one, without fail. Your weeping will turn into laughing.

Do not base your opinions on your current circumstances. Some people assume that because they are broke, they have done something wrong, and God is unhappy with them. That is not true. It is just a season, a "broke season." God has allowed this season to test your faith. Your faith will take you into the next season, and it will remove you from your present season. You have not put your faith in your money anyway, have you? You have put your faith in the God who is much more permanent than money. This season, too, shall pass.

Here is God's promise to Noah and to all of us who have followed after Him:

> *As long as the earth endures,*
> > *seedtime and harvest,*
> > *cold and heat,*
> > *summer and winter,*
> > *day and night*
> > *will never cease*
> (Genesis 8:22).

I rest my case.

Kingdom people are seasonal people. They do not worry when the sky grows dark. They know it will be all right in the long run. They know where to put their trust. They get a lot of practice putting it in the One who invented the seasons.

The Kingdom Economy—a Seasonal Perspective

What I am trying to say is that the economy of the Kingdom is seasonal. Seasons of crisis occur, and so do seasons without crisis. You need to move with them, maintaining a growing faith in the King. He is a Rock. Like a great boulder with waves breaking over it, He is immovable. He is our Father. He takes care of us.

In the Kingdom economy, the citizens of the Kingdom do not worry. Jesus knew that people have a tendency to worry. That is why He spent extra time talking about why worry is an unnecessary element in the economy of the Kingdom of Heaven:

Therefore I tell you, do not worry about your life, what you will eat or drink; or about your body, what you will wear. Is not life more important than food, and the body more important than clothes? Look at the birds of the air; they do not sow or reap or store away in barns, and yet your heavenly Father feeds them. Are you not much more valuable than they? Who of you by worrying can add a single hour to his life?

And why do you worry about clothes? See how the lilies of the field grow. They do not labor or spin. Yet I tell you that not even Solomon in all his splendor was dressed like one of these. If that is how God clothes the grass of the field, which is here today and tomorrow is thrown into the fire, will He not much more clothe you, O you of little faith? So do not worry, saying, "What shall we eat?" or "What shall we drink?" or "What shall we wear?" For the pagans run after all these things, and your heavenly Father knows that you need them. But seek first His kingdom and His righteousness, and all these things will be given to you as well. Therefore do not worry about tomorrow, for tomorrow will worry about itself. Each day has enough trouble of its own (Matthew 6:25-34).

You don't want to be like the pagans, do you? The verse above reads, "For the pagans run after all these things [worrying about the details of their lives], and your heavenly Father knows that you need them." The pagans get anxious and fearful and depressed. They panic. They can't sleep at night. They do not have anybody they can trust.

You do. Your trust is in God Himself. Therefore it does not matter when the storms blow in. You know two important facts: God is in charge, and He will take care of you. He always has, and He always will. Even if a crisis is a new one to you, it is not a new one to Him. He knows the end from the beginning. He will take this time of sorrow and turn it into a time of rejoicing. That's how His economy works.

Faith and Work

In the Kingdom economy, *faith* and *work* go hand in hand. Your faith as a citizen of the Kingdom is *active*. You have replaced the un-faith you had when you were a pagan (which was really worry), with action-filled faith.

Some people mistakenly think that "faith" is passive. They think that the less they do, the better. That is not what the apostle James thought. He encouraged people to support their faith in God with hard work. He wanted faith and work to be combined:

> *What good is it, my brothers, if a man claims to have faith but has no deeds? Can such faith save him? Suppose a brother or sister is without clothes and daily food. If one of you says to him, "Go, I wish you well; keep warm and well fed," but does nothing about his physical needs, what good is it? In the same way, faith by itself, if it is not accompanied by action, is dead* (James 2:14-17).

James had a very low opinion of people who merely believe in God. As he put it, "Even the demons believe that" (James 2:19). He expected people's faith, which is invisible, to result in visible actions, in things that show: "As the body without the spirit is dead, so faith without deeds is dead" (James 2:26). You cannot overcome a crisis by faith alone.

If you believe that God will bring you through this season of crisis, then get to work while you are waiting. He has things for you to do.

Work and Unity

In the Kingdom economy, people find unity in a time of crisis. This goes along with work because people find unity when they work together. You cannot help your neighbor without developing a degree of unity and a sense of community.

In a time of crisis, there is always something to do. You do not have time to pick and choose what you want to do or what person you want to do it with.

Let's say you and I live in the same apartment building. I live upstairs, and you live downstairs, but we don't speak to each other. In fact, we don't like each other very much. We merely tolerate each other. We have a bad attitude toward each other. All of a sudden one night, there is a fire. The apartment building catches on fire, and it is burning down. So I grab a bucket, and you grab a bucket. We start working together: "You get the water; I'll hold the bucket...." Our mutual crisis forces enemies to become friends. When the boat is sinking, everybody starts bailing. When the financial system is sinking, we help each other out.

A crisis creates a sense of community because when people are in trouble together, they have to get along. That is one of the good things about a bad situation.

Unity and Empathy

In a crisis, the Kingdom economy produces empathy. Sometimes you have been doing so well for so long that you do not know how to feel other people's hurt anymore. You become heartless toward other people.

God is doing you a favor when He allows you to lose some ground so that you can be reminded of how temporary your wealth is. When you are in a position to need help from other people for a change, you begin to appreciate them again. Your personal crisis brings you back to your humanity. You empathize. You love. You are willing to help people out. You enjoy the sense of solidarity that you had lost for a while. You may even start liking people again.

When a crisis comes, you have to deal with the simple basics of life. Maybe you used to spend all of your time seeking for "the finer things of life." The basics—food, shelter, etc.—just came to you automatically. You had no patience for the people who could not seem to provide for their families.

In any crisis, but especially in a financial crisis, you end up re-prioritizing your day-to-day life. You don't go shopping for a new iPod. You need to spend your money on food. You are not so busy anymore, so you have time to go to church. The crisis brings you back to spirituality. It brings you back to people. It brings you back to the things that count.

You have time to talk with your neighbor: "How are you doing?" That is not just a customary greeting. You mean it. Now you *care* how your neighbor is doing. He is looking out for you, and you are looking out for him.

New Perspectives

The way the seasons of crisis re-prioritize your life is simple: a crisis makes you understand what is important again.

Prosperity is dangerous in the sense that it can make you forget the source of it. God is the source of it, and sometimes God will back off so you can come back to Him. He will pull His hands back so you will come back looking for His hands again. He will allow you to experience the night so you can appreciate the daytime again.

Seasons of success cannot continue forever. If God let us live in success all of the time, we would forget about the main concerns of His Kingdom. He is not as interested in how much money you have in the bank as in what you are doing with it. He does not care about the title in front of your name as much as He cares about your heart. So He allows seasons of success to alternate with seasons of failure. Doors that were open get closed. Things that were healthy get sick.

It shakes you up, but that shaking will show you what is important. It may redirect you if you need to be redirected. A crisis places demands on your hidden potential. A crisis reveals your true beliefs and your convictions. It will show you what is "shakable" and what is not. The things that are situated on the Rock will not shake; they will only grow stronger and better.

You may call it a terrible experience, but God says that it is just a little blip on His screen. To Him, it is just an incident. You know, don't you, that a crisis on earth is merely an incident in Heaven? It is a matter of perspective.

What you see as a crisis, God sees as an opportunity for growth. What you see as humiliating, He sees as an occasion for the development of humble leadership. It is all in how you see it. What is your perspective?

Your perspective will keep you from staying stuck in a hole. The country of the Bahamas is made up of islands. For a long time, one of those islands was called Hog Island. Somebody named it that, and it was on the map that way. Then a guy came along and said, "I don't like that name. It is not a good name," and he renamed the island Paradise Island. Now you see Paradise Island on the map. When it was Hog Island, it was farmland. Now it has some of the most expensive real estate in the country.

When I was growing up in a poor family, I read this proverb, and it made me angry: "Rich and poor have this in common: The Lord is the Maker of them all" (Prov. 22:2). To me, that meant that God made rich people and God made poor people, and the problem was, I was one of the poor ones, and that was the end of the matter. I was angry at God because He had not made me one of the rich ones.

I kept on reading. The next verse talks about perspective: "A prudent man sees danger and takes refuge, but the simple keep going and suffer for it" (Prov. 22:3). In other words, depending upon how a person *sees,* so he interprets his situation. Feeling poor is a product of how you see life. So is feeling rich. And the next verse wraps it up: "Humility and the fear of the Lord bring wealth and honor and life" (Prov. 22:4).

Crisis and Opportunity

Not only is it important to interpret your current situation accurately, on Kingdom terms, but it is equally important to be able to see opportunities and to seize them. I remember a true story of two young men who were attending the University of Southern California together. They decided to take a trip together during their summer break. So they saved up their money to go to India, and they spent the whole summer there with their backpacks on, taking trains and seeing the cities and the countryside.

They saw millions of poor people. They had never seen such poverty before. They had never seen such filth. They were overwhelmed. One day, they were in a hostel, and one of the guys looked out of a second-story window. As far as his eyes could see, he saw poverty-stricken Indian people. They were barefoot, living in the mud. The men had no shirts on, and the children were naked. Flies were swarming and crawling all over them.

He said to his friend, "Gosh, man, look at all the poor people. They don't have any shoes on, and they don't even have clothes."

His buddy came to the window. He said, "Yeah, man, wow. What a place for a shoe business." That's all he said.

The two guys went back home and returned to college. They were both in the same classes. They were both studying business administration. As the second guy sat in class, he could not get the pictures of India out of his mind. He saw all those bare feet. So he started sketching on a piece of paper in the back of the class.

He ended up designing a pair of shoes that could be made out of plastic and mass-produced. He decided to drop out of school, against people's advice, because he had become obsessed with this idea about shoes for India. His friend said to him, "You are crazy. You've got to stay in school and get a job so you can make a living."

But the guy had this idea, and he was going to see what he could do with it. So he got somebody to make a prototype, and he found a company that said they could produce it for

15 cents a pair. He went to his brother's friend for start-up financing. His brother's friend said, "Do you have a market for these shoes?"

"Yes, I have a market—millions of barefoot Indians. I've got a big market in India. If we make this shoe for 15 cents, we can ship it over there and sell it for 50 cents, and we could get a shoe business going." His brother's friend thought that sounded good.

Within 12 months, they had produced over 3 million pairs of shoes, and they shipped them to some of the big cities in India. The guy became a millionaire in one year. He never did go back to school. When his friend graduated the following year, he hired him to be his accountant.

You see, the difference between those two young guys was in what they could *see* out that window. Both of them had the same scene in front of them—acres of barefoot people. But whereas one guy saw only poor, barefoot men, women, and children, the other guy saw something else—a way to help the people and a way to step up higher himself. One saw a crisis situation; the other saw an opportunity instead. It was a matter of perspective, vision, and hard work.

One saw a human need, and he figured out a way to help meet it. If you are in a time of financial crisis right now, look around you to see where you can meet a human need. Human needs never change. No matter what the environment, humans need certain things, and if you can get yourself involved in meeting human needs, your financial crisis will be a temporary one. Everywhere in the world, people need water, food, clothing—and security.

Have you observed that when the economy falls apart, certain types of jobs do not go away? They are the jobs that meet human needs: jobs in the medical profession and agriculture, jobs that offer counseling, emotional help—and funeral services. The jobs that depend on luxury goods and services may go away. But even in a bad economy, people have to eat. They may not be able to go to a five-star restaurant, but they will consider fast food.

The Inherent Seed

God will give you ideas, and He will give you the ability to work. He will let your world be shaken so that the seeds will shake out. He put seeds in your mind and heart. He wants them to grow. This may be your season for planting something new. Your seed is your purpose and your passion. We will talk some more about it in the next chapter, but for now I want you to understand the connection between *seasons* and *seeds*.

Inherent in a season of crisis and turmoil and drought is the seed of a season of plenty. After you find your seed, work the soil, and plant it, the rainy season will come and water it. Your seed will grow into a fine plant.

In every seed there is a forest. God's purposes are inside you, and all it takes is the right combination of crisis-time shaking and faith in God's Word to make you plant that seed. You were born with the natural talents to do something that the world needs, and God wants you to see the highway of opportunity inside you, even though you may feel as if you are on a dead-end path.

What is your seed right now? It may be that idea that won't go away, the thing you keep thinking about doing. (If you have been thinking about robbing a bank, however, I would start thinking about something else.)

You were born with seeds inside you, and you were born with jobs to do. Your future isn't out there in front of you someplace; it is trapped inside of you. Let the crisis time shake it loose. Take it and plant it with faith and work. Give yourself away. Link up with other people. Wait for the season to change.

Psalm 1 illustrates how people can grow in the right season:

Blessed is the man
>*who does not walk in the counsel of the wicked*
>*or stand in the way of sinners*
>*or sit in the seat of mockers.*

But his delight is in the law of the Lord,
>*and on His law he meditates day and night.*

He is like a tree planted by streams of water,
>*which yields its fruit in season*
>*and whose leaf does not wither.*
>*Whatever he does prospers*
>(Psalm 1:1-3).

Even for a tree planted by streams of water, there is a season when there is not any fruit. You may be living a righteous life, working hard, but not seeing any results. You may be "leafed out" well, but nobody can eat your leaves. You will think, *My faith is still grounded. My roots are still by the water of life. I am working hard. I am still alive, but I am not bearing any fruit.*

I promise you that there will be a season when you can feed others. Fruitfulness is a seasonal benefit. You just keep growing.

Seeds are never in a recession. They never hesitate to grow, given the right conditions. Even in Haiti, which is the poorest country in the Western Hemisphere, the seeds grow just fine. If you plant a seed in Haiti, most likely it will grow.

The season will change. A fruitful growing season is coming. Your present crisis condition is not permanent. God says so:

I will bless them and the places surrounding My hill. I will send down showers in season; there will be showers of blessing. The trees of the field will yield their fruit and the ground will yield its crops; the people will be secure in their land. They will know that I am the Lord, when I break the bars of their yoke and rescue them from the hands of those who enslaved them. They will no longer be plundered by the nations, nor will wild animals devour them. They will live in safety, and no one will make them afraid (Ezekiel 34:26-28).

CHAPTER 6

The Seed Principle

Seeds of faith are always within us; sometimes it takes a crisis to nourish and encourage their growth.
—Susan Taylor

In a time of crisis—or any time—the secret to thriving is to understand the secret of being fruitful. The secret of being fruitful is best understood in terms of what I call the Seed Principle.

This goes back to Adam and Eve in the Garden, where God told human beings how He wanted them to live on the earth. Chapter 3 was about how God gave Adam what I call the Management Mandate for humanity. What did He say? God told Adam, "Be fruitful. Multiply. Reproduce. Replenish. Subdue and have dominion over everything that I have created." (See Genesis 1:28.) God had given Adam something to manage—the Garden, which was filled with the plants and the creatures that God had just created. They could not take care of themselves. Adam could not neglect them. He needed to care for them and to help them to be as fruitful as possible.

Adam stepped forward and began to learn what this might mean. He had never seen a plant or a tree before, and he had no idea about how they bore fruit or that inside each fruit was a seed that contained the DNA to reproduce the plant it came from. He did not even know that he could eat the fruit until God told him. But it did not take him long to learn that part of his management job meant taking care of the seeds; otherwise, the green, growing things could not reproduce themselves and be fruitful. In terms of plants and trees, it was not long before Adam knew what it meant to "multiply" and "reproduce" and "replenish." Although he didn't really understand it, when he and his wife produced first one son, Cain, and then another, Abel, the same "seed principle" was at work. This was God's pattern for life.

Be Fruitful

Many, many generations later, God looks at you, and He says, simply, "Be fruitful." He doesn't ask you to go and find seed someplace. His assumption is that you are carrying the seed already. There are 6.7 billion seed containers on the earth today, and one of them is sitting in your chair right now. You did not come to earth empty. God will never demand what He does not supply. He will never request what He has not first instilled.

Which comes first, the seed or the fruit? The seed. But God does not say, "Be seed-full." He expects the seed to grow up into a fruit-bearing plant, so He says, "Be fruitful." He is implying that He has given you seed. He is implying that you are carrying something with which you can reproduce life. It is in you.

Now I am not talking only about children. I am talking about your future, which is in you in seed form. In fact, your future fruitfulness is already starting to sprout. Can you feel it? If it is in the right environment, it will grow fast. Living in the Kingdom of God is the best environment of all for fruitfulness and growth. If you do a good job of managing the growth of your seed (which entails obedience to the Master Gardener), you will be able to grow into your full, mature, Kingdom potential. You will fulfill the purpose for which He created you.

That is true fruitfulness!

Multiply

In the Bahamas, if you plant one mango seed, you will never get just one mango back. You will get hundreds of them. Thousands. You will get the same kind of fruit you started with, but it will be multiplied a thousandfold. That seed possesses attributes. One of those attributes is multiplication.

Each seed carries life within itself. Each seed carries the potential for increase. Each seed produces after its own kind. Each seed is gift from God. In the right environment, with a little God-supplied management, the seed can grow and mature and bear fruit. The old seed did not produce the mature fruit for itself. The old seed has disappeared in the process. Now all you see is the multiplied fruit of the original seed. And the new fruit bears new seed as it matures.

I'll never forget what Oral Roberts, my father in the faith, said to us back in 1976 in chapel at Oral Roberts University. He said, "When you can't meet your need, turn it into a seed." As a student, I took hold of that word. I was not able to pay my tuition. So I took what little money I had left, and I took it to the front of the chapel for an offering. I said, "God, I can't pay my tuition anyhow, so I might as well give it."

Do you know what happened? Two days later an envelope appeared from nowhere in my mailbox with twice as much money as I was going to need for tuition. That's what I call multiplication! I sowed some seed, and it multiplied in answer to my prayer.

The Gift of Seed

By means of the Seed Principle, God sustains life. If the seeds are managed properly, life will not die out. Season after season, everything will grow and bear more fruit.

Jesus taught us to pray, "Give us this day our daily bread," but as you know, God doesn't have any bread growing on trees. He does not give us bread outright; He gives us seed. He gives us wheat, oats, barley, and other kinds of seeds that reproduce enough seed kernels to be put through a grinding process to make flour, which is then made into bread.

It is good to know this when we pray for something and His answer does not seem to resemble what we prayed for. We know God does not make mistakes. Could it be that He has supplied us with the *seed* we need? Could it be that we need to patiently tend the seed until it reproduces? Could some kind of grinding (in the form of crises) be involved in the process of producing, at long last, the thing you prayed for?

You prayed for money, and He gave you a job. Well, there you go; your hard work is the cultivation process. You will reap the money you prayed for. You prayed for the harvest, the end product. That is not a bad thing to pray for. But do not be surprised when the answer you get is in the form of harvest-producing seed. God may deploy you to sow some seed and to take care of it until it grows up. Then you can have your harvest, and with it comes the idea of sowing some more seed.

You prayed that you would be a true citizen of the Kingdom. Instead of transforming you instantly into a fully mature believer, He just sent you a crisis. What is happening? Out of the midst of the fire, He intends to purify you. He wants you to come out shiny and strong, so that you can, like a true citizen of the Kingdom, reproduce Kingdom life generously. Look at this passage of Scripture, which pulls it all together:

> *Now He who supplies seed to the sower and bread for food will also supply and increase your store of seed and will enlarge the harvest of your righteousness. You will be made rich in every way so that you can be generous on*

every occasion, and through us your generosity will result in thanksgiving to God (2 Corinthians 9:10-11).

You see what I mean. God does not give you ready-to-eat bread. He gives you seed. This shows that He is a wise Father. You know as well as I do what happens when we just give a handout of bread to a beggar. It may take care of him for one day, but what about tomorrow? Once he eats the bread, he is back to begging for more. Far better to help that beggar earn a living so he can acquire his own bread. It may take quite awhile, but it will be a better result.

If I give you one seed, it will reproduce and multiply and provide food for you as long as you need it. It will enable you to be generous, so you can "seed into" someone else's life. That is how it works with God, too.

Being Seed-Full

I mentioned that your "seed" is more than your ability to produce children; it is also your innate potential, which is meant to lead to the destiny for which God created you. Everyone possesses some kind of a seed. That seed is a seed of potential, purpose, and passion. That seed contains your future. As I said in the previous chapter, "In every seed there is a forest."

Do not allow it to remain a mere seed. It is important for you to find it, plant it, and nurture it to maturity. Assuming that you do this, your seed will multiply greatly.

That seed inside you is your *ideas*. You pray for bread, and God gives you an idea. You pray for money, and God gives you an idea. You pray for more resources, and God gives you another idea.

If you are paying attention and not being lazy like so many Christians are—as they sit around, waiting for a miracle to happen—you will be able to catch on that God has already supplied the seeds for your miracle.

For example, you ask God for more promotion, and He gives you an idea. He suggests, "I'll tell you what to do: come to work earlier and leave later, but do not ask for overtime pay. Let them see your dedication."

"Oh no, God," you say. "I didn't say I wanted to do something like that. I just want a promotion. I want more money."

God says, "You didn't listen to Me. I just gave you a seed. Now go and plant it." It is not enough to be "seed-full." The seed is not the fruit. You need to do something with your seed.

You will not get very far if you abort the process. Do not become like the beggar, who runs out of provision daily. He doesn't seem to want to take hold of the seed inside him, since he never plants it. After awhile, it becomes even more impossible for him to exert himself in this regard.

Being seed-full involves creativity. It is part of the definition of a seed to be creative—to create new life, to reproduce itself. Tucked away inside yourself, you have seeds from which new life can be created. The critical step is to lay hold of that seed—that idea—and to do something with it. Far too often, people do not do that.

I am telling you, one of the best environments for creativity is an environment of crisis. During a crisis is when you get motivated to change. That is when you cry out to God in prayer. That is when you pay attention to what He tells you.

When you find yourself in a time of crisis, do not assume that your fruitfulness is at risk. Far from being at risk, it is about to increase. In a time of crisis, you will look harder for good ideas. You will assess your natural talents. You will be willing to work a little harder and a little longer. You will not tend to be lazy because you will be motivated to get out of the uncomfortable crisis situation. You will not be as afraid of taking a risk because you will have less to lose.

Therefore, never underestimate the value of a crisis. Imitate your Father. When the earth was "without form, and void"—chaos—He got creative. He planted seeds. He is still doing it today, through people like you and me. At His direction, we can take a chaotic crisis (a mess) and turn it into a "bless." You can take a lack and turn it into a "plenty."

Your Future Seed

The key to your life is discovering and developing and serving your seed gift. I want to help you do this because I want people to be able to eat of your fruit.

Some people will actually pay to get the fruit that you offer. They will really want what you have to give. When you go to a certain gas station to fuel up your car, you do not go there primarily because you like the guy who owns the gas station, but because he has something to offer that you need. You are willing to pay him so that you can have what he offers. That guy won't have to worry about a depressed economy depriving him of his livelihood because he is supplying something that people really need. People don't drink gasoline, but their cars do, and they want their cars to function. Somehow, they will find a way to afford gasoline. His "fruit" attracts people's resources, their money. His fruit will never be in recession.

When you find your seed and grow your fruit, you will start to feel fulfilled. You will be fulfilling your purpose, and you will be satisfying your passion. You will have found what you were born with, and you will have stepped into the future that God intended for you.

You will always have what you were born with, even if you do not discover it until you are 99 years old. Your seed is impossible to lose.

But how sad it is when people reach the end of a long life, and they never did anything with their seed. They just existed. They made it; they survived. They may have produced a few children, but they did not reproduce Kingdom life. Their future destiny remained trapped inside of them for all those years. Even when the storms of crisis came and the wildfires of crisis burned, they didn't get it. They thought it was somebody else's job to overcome the crisis. The whole time, they never understood that the crisis may have been

God's way of getting their attention. They never comprehended that the crisis was supposed to modify them and mold them into the people God created them to be.

People who miss their future are everywhere. Most of the people you know may be those kind of people. They are like ants, toiling away all day long for a crumb. Even when God tried to jolt them awake, they remained asleep to their potential. It's not as if God didn't try. He's trying all the time to wake them up. He has hidden their future right under their noses; He does not want them to miss it.

However, when it comes in an unpleasant package—a crisis, for instance—people have a way of closing their eyes. They cannot get past the immediate circumstances. They certainly cannot locate the new and innovative ideas that are still in seed form in their hearts and minds. (By the way, I believe that our educational system and our demanding careers play a strong negative role in burying our awareness of what God created us to do. We are taught to follow a particular wellworn path. We are not taught to follow our passions. Most of our choices in schooling and career center around somebody else's idea of what is good for us. We choose careers based on monetary interests rather than personal fulfillment. We can only tell after the whole thing collapses, and we are left with no sense of fulfillment.)

The people who find and fulfill their God-given destiny are most likely to be believers, especially the ones who take the Word to heart and who want God to help them grow. Those are the people who have eyes to see the little seeds that have not even germinated yet. They are the ones who can identify the gifts God has given them and who can obey God's promptings to follow their passions.

Although it is true that nobody can take your gift from you (your seed), you are the one who is in charge of what happens with it. You have free will. You can choose to uncover your gift, cultivate it, develop it, refine it. Or not.

If you do not do anything with it, it will remain dormant inside you. No one can take it from you, but you will be guilty of hoarding your seed. God will have to find someone else to do the thing He created you to do. Someone else will have the wonderful experience of finding fulfillment and of being able to offer the world something unique.

I said before that your seed will grow best in the right environment. I am trying to provide you with a "fertilizer" environment in the pages of this book. You will not have to manipulate the seed inside you to make it grow. If you allow the right conditions to prevail, that seed will just begin to sprout on its own. You will be like a mango seed with a whole tree inside. Once it lands in the right soil, here comes a tree.

I am also trying to provide you with a perspective on the circumstances of your life, both the good ones and the bad ones. Fertilizer smells bad sometimes—have you noticed? This bad-smelling crisis that you have just landed in may be the perfect environment for growing your seed. All you may need is permission.

The purposes of your heart are like a deep well full of water, and you need a little help to pull them out. (See

Proverbs 20:5.) You need some encouragement, and you need permission. Then you will be free to pull away everything that is hindering that seed from growing

What Do You Have?

Look inside. Ask God to shine His light in there. What do you see? Does anything look like a seed? What do you have?

When God asked Moses that question, the results were miraculous:

The Lord said to him, "What is that in your hand?"

"A staff," he replied.

The Lord said, "Throw it on the ground."

Moses threw it on the ground and it became a snake, and he ran from it.

Then the Lord said to him, "Reach out your hand and take it by the tail." So Moses reached out and took hold of the snake and it turned back into a staff in his hand.

"This," said the Lord, "is so that they may believe that the Lord, the God of their fathers—the God of Abraham, the God of Isaac and the God of Jacob—has appeared to you" (Exodus 4:2-5).

When Elisha asked the widow that question, the results were equally miraculous:

The wife of a man from the company of the prophets cried out to Elisha, "Your servant my husband is dead, and you know

that he revered the Lord. But now his creditor is coming to take my two boys as his slaves."

Elisha replied to her, "How can I help you? Tell me, what do you have in your house?"

"Your servant has nothing there at all," she said, "except a little oil."

Elisha said, "Go around and ask all your neighbors for empty jars. Don't ask for just a few. Then go inside and shut the door behind you and your sons. Pour oil into all the jars, and as each is filled, put it to one side."

She left him and afterward shut the door behind her and her sons. They brought the jars to her and she kept pouring. When all the jars were full, she said to her son, "Bring me another one."

But he replied, "There is not a jar left." Then the oil stopped flowing.

She went and told the man of God, and he said, "Go, sell the oil and pay your debts. You and your sons can live on what is left" (2 Kings 4:1-7).

What do *you* have? Assess yourself. Look inside, and ask God to help you see with His eyes.

Do you have an idea for a business? Have you been thinking about that idea for a long time? Go for it. See if you can take the next steps. Come up with a business plan. Evaluate your idea for a product or a service. Is it something that people will pay for? Decide what kind of support structure you will need. See if you can get the right people interested in your idea.

If you can get the seed of your idea to sprout, that is good, but it is not over yet. In fact, it is only the beginning. Now you need to enter into a long stretch of hard work. Get adjusted to the concept that you may be working hard for the rest of your life.

Stay connected to God. It is too easy to let your work become your god. Allow Him to give you course corrections. Submit yourself to people who can give you wise advice.

Be generous. Sow a little seed here and there. Be faithful to tithe. Even as you are careful and sensible, do not hoard your growing resources.

You know what will happen in due time; you will have a prosperous business. You will be able to support more than yourself and your family. Your employees and your customers alike will benefit from what started out as a mere seed of an idea inside you.

See Beyond Your Eyes

What do you have? The people of the world are actually looking for your seed. The world needs your seed, but it needs to be in fruit form. When you go to a mango tree, do you go to eat the seed? No, you go for the fruit. Nobody eats mango seeds; people eat mango fruit. You can't get enough nutrients from one little seed. As food it is useless. You can't eat one seed for a meal. Not even a bird can make a meal out of one little seed. Yet that is how most of us are. We exist. When roll call comes, we can reply, "Present! Here!" Then we sink back into our seats and wait for someone else to do something.

Each one of us has got to bear fruit. You have got to bear the first fruit. You have got to get pregnant (yes, even if you are male!). You have got to become a solution. You were born to solve a problem on the earth. You are God's response to a need in the world. You are the answer to a question that God knew would be asked in your generation. You are the fulfillment of one of God's desires. There is something that He wanted done, and that made you necessary. He created you for something.

He did not create you just to make a living somehow, pay the bills, and die. He did not need to create somebody else to take up space and use up oxygen. He created you to deliver something of His Kingdom to the earth. He created you to answer a question. He created you to make a contribution. He created you to become a carrier of His ideas, His seeds, so you could become part of His creative team.

You are a necessary part of His plan.

Do not put yourself down. Do not assume that this means someone else. No, you yourself are a necessary part of God's plan on the earth today. It does not matter what kind of a background you have. After all, Jesus called Matthew to be His disciple, and Matthew was a tax collector, which was not much better than being a criminal in those days. (See Matthew 9:9; 21:31-32; Mark 2:14; Luke 5:27; 7:34.)

Do not go around thinking that God cannot use you just because you were not born into the "right" family in the "right" country. That is very much like our odd tendency to think that anything foreign is better than what we have right now. If somebody has a foreign accent, especially certain ones, or if they come from a famous city (preferably a wealthy and cultured city), or if they appear to be a bit exotic, we consider that person, or the products recommended by that person, to be superior.

You may come from a very ordinary background. You may appear in a very ordinary package, and you may not think that you have anything in particular to recommend you. But God created you, and that means He gave you some special purpose. When you start to walk in that purpose, you will start to feel fulfilled.

Do you remember the disciple named Andrew from the Bible? Andrew has no Gospel book named after him. He is only mentioned a few times. But Andrew was a very necessary part of God's plan. He and his brother Peter were fishermen, and they left their nets when they heard Jesus calling their names. They were the very first disciples. Almost every time Andrew is mentioned, it is "Andrew and…" or "…and Andrew." By himself, he does not seem to be very special.

However, Andrew's gift was networking—and I don't mean working his fishing nets. Andrew was vital to God's plan. According to the Gospel of John, Andrew was the one who went to tell Peter about Jesus:

Andrew, Simon Peter's brother, was one of the two who heard what John had said and who had followed Jesus. The first thing Andrew did was to find his brother

Simon and tell him, "We have found the Messiah" (that is, the Christ). And he brought him to Jesus... (John 1:40-42).

What Andrew did was very important for the Kingdom of God. It may have seemed like a small thing, but he seemed to do it consistently. He introduced people to their Savior. Some of those people, like Peter, who became the head of the Church, turned out to have enormous roles to play in the Kingdom of God. What if Andrew had decided that his career was more important than Jesus' call? What if both of the brothers had decided that they could not abandon the family business, which was fishing, to follow this rabbi who claimed they were supposed to start "fishing for men"? (See Matthew 4:19 and Mark 1:17.) We just might not be here today....

Take What You Have, and Let God Multiply It

When the disciples were confronted with a major dilemma—how to feed more than 5,000 people—Jesus asked them what they had on hand to feed the people with. It did not look like much. In fact, it was as insufficient as a handful of seeds in a hungry city. They could almost hear thousands of stomachs growling. The people, who had listened to Jesus all day long in the hot sun, were weak with hunger.

As evening approached, the disciples came to Him and said, "This is a remote place, and it's already getting late. Send the crowds away, so they can go to the villages and buy themselves some food."

Jesus replied, "They do not need to go away. You give them something to eat."

"We have here only five loaves of bread and two fish," they answered.

"Bring them here to me," He said. And He directed the people to sit down on the grass. Taking the five loaves and the two fish and looking up to heaven, He gave thanks and broke the loaves. Then He gave them to the disciples, and the disciples gave them to the people (Matthew 14:15-19).

That is a true story, and it was not written for "someone else." It was written for you. You may feel as insignificant as the little lad who donated his five small loaves of bread and two dried-up fish, but look what God can do with seed like that!

CHAPTER 7

The Secret to Thriving in a Time of Crisis

Most of life's battles are fought inside ourselves, and our greatest periods of growth usually come during crises. —*Robert Scheid*

The secret to thriving (not just surviving) in a time of crisis is effective management. Let me repeat that, with emphasis: The *secret to thriving* (not just surviving) in a time of crisis is *effective management*.

I am not trying to get on your nerves by reducing everything to statements about "effective management." While that may sound like a dull phrase, the reality behind it is far from dull. Yes, effective management itself is mostly a secret, hidden thing, noticeable more when it is missing than when it is operating effectively and smoothly. I will admit that unless you happen to be writing (or reading) a book about it, or unless your pastor or your business guru has decided to teach about it, you probably will not think much about "effective management," per se.

But when you have a time of crisis, the secret gets exposed. There is only one way out of a crisis—good management. You have to manage your way out of your crisis, and other people will be watching you. Even if they do not know what to call it, they can see you in action. They will be watching while you manage your way out of your crisis, and they will be able to tell whether you did it effectively or not. They will be able to tell whether you are barely surviving your crisis—or actually thriving in the midst of it.

Certainly, other people can see it when you manage your crisis *in*effectively. That is when you almost fail to emerge from crisis mode. That's when you stay in a crisis for a long time, stewing and fretting and getting too depressed to exert enough energy to break out. If that is you, I am sorry to say that it is not effective management. It is some kind of management—limited management, inadequate management, incompetent management—but I would not call it effective management. Effective management gets you going. Effective management gets you unstuck. Effective management takes you someplace. Effective management can become exciting—especially in a time of crisis.

Who are the people who seem like heroes in a time of crisis? They are the ones who were prepared, even though often they did not realize ahead of time that they were getting prepared for a crisis. How did they end up getting prepared? Simply by living their lives the way God intended, in accord with His principles and in obedience to His commandments.

What does "obedience to His commandments" mean? As you already know, in this book I am not referring so much to the Ten Commandments of Moses or to any other set of commandments that can be found in the Bible, but largely to the foundational commandments of God, the earliest commandments that God ever uttered to humankind, commandments that He has never rescinded or amended. These are His original commands to "be fruitful," to "multiply," and to "subdue the earth." That's what He told Adam and Eve to do, and it holds true to this very moment. He Himself continues to be in charge of the operation of the entire universe, and He has handed over the management of the operations of the earth to human helpers.

That includes you and me. He wants us to look to Him for day-to-day and year-to-year guidance. He wants us to take our marching orders straight from His throne. He wants us to consult with each other and to collaborate together. If we follow His guidance for the details, walking the straight and narrow path that He sets out before us (see Matt. 7:13-14), we will see good results.

This foundational set of commandments from God is a command, or mandate, to manage the resources of the earth. It undergirds everything that we do. If we are obedient to this simple set of commands to the best of our faith-filled ability, we will be prepared for whatever comes our way. We will be effective managers, and we will be the most likely people to thrive in any crisis.

God as Boss

God gave human beings the responsibility to manage the earth's resources, but He will always own the resources. In the Kingdom of God, nobody owns anything except God. Human beings were given dominion and "managership," not ownership.

Dominion over the earth's resources is our primary assignment. Once we lay hold of this fact, the purpose of our lives becomes clear. No longer do we need to get anxious about having enough money or food or any other kind of resource. Our job is to manage the resources, not to generate them.

Yet, being part of God's Kingdom does not guarantee us a free ride. Ever since God put forward His divinely inspired goal of having humans extend the culture of Heaven on the earth through the cooperation of Kingdom citizens such as you and me, the task has involved *work*. Adam worked the soil to tend the Garden. Laboring and sweating, he managed the resources God had provided.

That is still true today. Each one of us, separately and together, needs to labor and sweat to manage the resources of the earth. By means of our toil, we reap the fruit we need to sustain our lives and to carry on the effort. The more effective our work (management), the more resources God will give us. In other words, the more effective our management, the more growth we will enjoy. The more growth we enjoy, the more fruit we will reap. The more fruit we will reap, the more of God's Kingdom will be established on the earth.

God will not trust you with more than you can manage. He simply prevents growth where there is no management. He did not send the rain to water the Garden until He had created Adam to manage the growth that would result from it. God will not allow development where there is no management. God will not allow anything to expand unless He has a man or a woman who will manage that development.

God's primary measure of trusting you is management. Through your faithfulness and through your faith, God's Kingdom gets extended, one person at a time. Through your effective management, the necessary resources come to hand. Your effective management attracts more resources so that you can keep on fulfilling your purpose, come what may.

Crises Coming and Going

A huge part of effective management is being able to manage the crises that will happen—and crises are inevitable. Any business manager knows this, and so does any parent. If you are going to crumble in the face of a crisis, everything you are responsible for is going to crumble as well.

Because it is so important to manage crises as well as possible, I expanded these ideas in Chapter 4, where I call them "Seven Ways to Manage a Crisis":

1. Determine what your *needs* are (list them). Do not confuse your "wants" with needs.

2. Only acquire what you truly *need*.

3. Decide not to live beyond your ability.

4. Withdraw from the unnecessary.

5. Delay major projects.

6. Value your possessions.

7. Save, conserve, and protect your resources.

I believe that we need to review these crisis-management techniques every time we encounter a new crisis. As human beings, we all tend to have trouble thinking straight when a crisis hits. It seems to be a part of any crisis to have a "management crisis" at the same time.

When a crisis hits, you need to review what you have learned from previous crises, as well as what you have learned from outside sources (such as this book). You will need to remember that each one of us is a "mixed bag," always. Nobody is perfect. The whole idea is to keep learning more about how to live in faith, God's way, and to keep maturing as a citizen of the Kingdom.

When a crisis comes down on top of your head, you may well discover some things that you were doing *right* all along. Praise God for that! Maybe this time, you really were living within your means, so even though the bottom has fallen out of the job market and you are unemployed, you do not have to contend with debts. Maybe you will have acquired what you truly need, so now you will not need to divest yourself of a lot of extra stuff.

But I guarantee you that before this crisis ends, you will have learned some new things. Praise God for that, too. He is your divine Shepherd, and He is making sure that you will be strong enough for the long trek ahead. He is using the circumstances of life to make you into more of a Kingdombringer.

The Money Mentality

I have said that "effective management attracts resources." As a crucial part of managing a crisis, we must identify which resources we truly need and then we must save, conserve, and protect those resources. Our effective management is expressed by means of effective saving, conserving, and protection of the resources that God has entrusted to us. In the long run, our effectiveness attracts more resources.

Sometimes, however, all the resources look as if they have vanished, especially monetary resources. Where did they go? They must be here somewhere. No money got shipped to the moon or to Mars. The billions must still be on earth somewhere. All the gold and silver must be hidden somewhere. It is up to Kingdom citizens to exercise effective management and to "manage" those monetary resources out of their hiding places.

God says, "I will give you the treasures of darkness, riches stored in secret places, so that you may know that I am the Lord, the God of Israel, who summons you by name" (Isa. 45:3). God says He will give you the riches stored in secret places—if you save, conserve, and protect (manage) the resources He has given you up to this time.

Managers get value for their dollars. Managers use their resources effectively, without waste. Then when a time of crisis comes, they keep on doing it. They manage their way right out of the crisis and "graduate" up a level. When the stock market crashes, they are in a position to buy up the cheap stock. When unemployment hits, they have a cushion in the bank. They were not living above their ability or from paycheck to paycheck. When a natural disaster or a health crisis hits, they have the saved-up resources they need to ride it out.

If you want God to bless your life, you need to learn how to manage the resources He has entrusted to you now. You need to look at your life through the practical lens of proverbs like the following one, which have a lot to say about conserving resources and money: "Ants are creatures of little strength, yet they store up their food in the summer" (Prov. 30:25). The ant saves in summer because in winter there will be no food. At this point in time, an economic "winter" is starting to come over our whole earth. Have you conserved your resources? Have you been an ant—or not? "Of what use is money in the hand of a fool, since he has no desire to get wisdom?" (Prov. 17:16).

You need to be a man or a woman of integrity, not a person who only pretends to have resources. Pretending to be wealthy doesn't buy you anything. What good is it to acquire a Rolls Royce and park it in front of a one-bedroom house? What do you think you are proving when you get a satellite dish that is bigger than the bedroom roof it is sitting on? That is pretense—and it is a foolish way to handle the money you do have. The writer of Proverbs puts it this way:

One man pretends to be rich, yet has nothing; another pretends to be poor, yet has great wealth (Proverbs 13:7).

Dishonest money dwindles away, but he who gathers money little by little makes it grow (Proverbs 13:11).

Next time you start to complain about not having enough money, consider this: except for the youngest child among us, almost all of us have already become millionaires at least once, and probably more than once, in our lifetimes. Yes, you are a multi-millionaire! You just don't have all of the money anymore. But you had it when you needed it, didn't you? It went through your hands. Millions of dollars have passed through your hands in some form.

And whenever a money crisis has hit, you have learned to turn to the Source again. He has always given you what He felt you could manage. He has been giving you management lessons. He is still doing that, and you are still learning. It can take awhile to grow up into full maturity as a citizen of the Kingdom of God.

The secret to thriving in times of crisis is the same as the secret to thriving in the non-crisis times. The secret is management, and effective management implies trust. Get your feet planted solidly on the Rock. It's worth any crisis you have to live through.

The Secret to Wealth

Just as currency varies from country to country, so wealth comes in different forms besides money. For the most part, the wealth of the earth comes in the form of all of the many resources that God has created for the earth.

We read in Genesis that "the Lord God made all kinds of trees grow out of the ground—trees that were pleasing to the eye and good for food..." (Gen. 2:9). The river that watered the Garden flowed from four separate headwaters. The first of the four rivers wound through a land where high-quality gold could be found. Aromatic resin and onyx were also found there (see Gen. 2:10-12).

Adam had already been established as the gardener, and he was able to appreciate one type of wealth—edible fruit. One type of wealth (food) comes from the soil by means of agriculture. He understood, too, that the reason the trees of the Garden flourished was because of the water furnished by the river. So water turns out to be another form of wealth. The tissues of the human body are more than half water. People cannot get along without water and food.

Moving outside the Garden itself, God was giving Adam and his descendents several other types of wealth as well. One was gold, which has been considered valuable since ancient times. By extension, other precious metals, such as silver, are also a form of wealth. Another form of wealth that is noteworthy to this day is oil (resin). Oil represents fuel for cooking, warmth, and, in modern times, transportation and industry. Last we have onyx, which represents precious stones of all types, including diamonds.

I call these the five foundations of wealth: (1) fruit or food; (2) water, for life support; (3) gold and other precious metals; (4) resin or oil for fuel; and (5) onyx and other precious stones. God gave each of these to Adam. In essence, God said, "Adam, I give you every fruit for food" (see Gen. 2:16). Then He said, "I give you water." Then, "I give you gold; I give you resin; I give you onyx." By giving them to Adam, God was giving them to us.

Because these five commodities are foundational, anyone who deals effectively in them will be able to become wealthy. When a time of crisis comes, people will revert to the foundational commodities. Which would you rather have in a time of crisis, a valley filled with vegetables or a silicon valley?

God gave beautiful advice to Adam; He started with agriculture and water. They are like the foundations of the foundations. After food and water are secured, then Adam could go digging in the ground for gold, oil, and precious stones.

When we reverse the priorities, we die for lack of food. We have discovered that the hard way, by making the last priorities first. Instead of taking good care of the resources that God gave to us, we have messed them up. We have fouled up the water and the soil with chemicals and erosion and over-cultivation. We have fought wars over gold, oil, and the other types of wealth. We keep going after things that human beings do not really need.

In a nutshell, we are greedy. We must keep coming back to greed as the reason for our economic crisis. People have desired more wealth than they could manage, and they have not been afraid to do harm to acquire it. They have confused their wants with their desires. The whole time they have divorced themselves from God who could have instructed them with wisdom and the ability to manage the resources they had at the beginning.

When we reverse the priorities, we mismanage the resources. And when we mismanage the resources, we lose them. A good part of the time, we are creating our own economic crises, don't you think?

When you find yourself in a time of financial instability, it may be the right time to sell your assets that are mere decorations. You paid $10,000 for that diamond, and then you put it in a drawer. Maybe now is the time to dig it out and turn it back into a liquid asset so you can buy food and water with it. Sometimes common sense provides the best kind of wisdom. It may be time to off-load some things, to withdraw from some of the complications of owning too many possessions, to get back to the basics of life.

The Power of Effective Management

The power of effective management can be summed up as effective dominance. *Dominance* does not have to be a bad word. When you dominate something, you are managing it. You can dominate (manage) with wisdom and restraint, and with self-sacrifice and love. The idea of dominance does not have to imply brutal force or unwelcome pressure. In fact, if everyone exercised the right kind of dominion, we would all have enough resources because, as I have already explained, effective management attracts more resources.

Dominance does not mean that a few people are in charge and that the rest of the people have to submit. When God told Adam: "Be fruitful. Multiply. Subdue the earth," He was summing up what it would take for Adam and his descendents to be effective in managing the resources of the earth.

In actual fact, God did not tell Adam to subdue the other *people* who would populate the earth. That kind of dominance is what has given the word a negative connotation. God told Adam to subdue the earth's *resources*. We are descended from Adam. Therefore, like him, we have the same assignment: Be fruitful. Multiply. Subdue the earth. And this means, "Manage the resources."

In the context of that universal purpose statement for all of humankind, God has given every single individual an assignment, a purpose. You have a part to play as much as I do. Each one of us has a part to play in bringing in the Kingdom of God on the earth.

Look at how The Message version of Genesis puts it:

God spoke: "Let us make human beings in Our image, make
them reflecting Our nature

So they can be responsible for the fish in the sea,
the birds in the air, the cattle,

And, yes, Earth itself,
> *and every animal that moves on the face of*
> *Earth."*

God created human beings;
> *He created them godlike,*

Reflecting God's nature.
> *He created them male and female.*

God blessed them:
> *"Prosper! Reproduce! Fill Earth! Take charge!*

Be responsible for fish in the sea and birds in the air,
> *for every living thing that moves on the face of*
> *Earth."*

Then God said, "I've given you
> *every sort of seed-bearing plant on Earth*

And every kind of fruit-bearing tree,
> *given them to you for food.*

To all animals and all birds,
> *everything that moves and breathes,*

I give whatever grows out of the ground for food."
> *And there it was.*

God looked over everything He had made;
> *it was so good, so very good!*
(Genesis 1:26-31 TM)

God created the first people to reflect His nature. He created resources so that they could survive and thrive. He wanted both the people and the resources to be multiplied to fill the earth. He wanted the culture of the earth to reflect the culture of Heaven, and that means that He wanted people to prosper. In order to prosper, they simply had to follow God's instructions to be fruitful, to multiply, and to subdue or dominate the earth.

Sounds simple, doesn't it? Yet, without even thinking very hard, you can start to get discouraged. By this time, everything in the world is so badly messed up. Where can you start to undo the mess? Everywhere you turn, you find a crisis—or a crisis in the making. Often, those crises were made by somebody else, and you cannot make another person (or country, or human culture) change, can you? Why should you even bother about it?

You cannot undo the past, but you can do something with your own life. In fact, your own life is all you have to offer.

Your Personal Assignment

What portion of the resources of the earth has God created you to manage, subdue, or dominate? He has given you some kind of an assignment because He has built into every human being a purpose, something to produce, something to reproduce.

Your assignment does not have to be gardening or farming or gathering food, as it was for Adam. Your assignment will use whatever natural and spiritual gifts God has given you. It will encompass the whole of your life, not only your career path. It may well be a collaborative assignment, something that will require you to work alongside other people, without whom you will not be able to accomplish your purpose. Most of our assignments are collaborative.

If you have a gift of musical talent, ask God what He wants you to do with it. Does He want you to sing by yourself in the shower, or does He want you to multiply your gift by reproducing your music on a CD? Does He want you to instruct and encourage budding musicians? Does He want you to coordinate the musical efforts of other people, thereby helping to fill the earth with music?

If you are supposed to have dominion over the earth, you must use what resources and gifts you started with and, with God's help, multiply and distribute them. You need to distribute goods and services. You cannot stockpile your goods in warehouses, literally or figuratively, or you may die of poverty, and so may the people who were supposed to receive your goods.

Any businessperson knows that the number one burden on business is inventory. Excess inventory is a business killer. Excess inventory means that your fruit is stored up instead of getting taken to market. Taking it to market is distribution (multiplication). Distributing it effectively is the same as subduing the market. If you subdue your market, you can control it, and you can take dominion in that market, which is a little corner of the earth.

Get Beyond Managing Your Crisis

So, whether you are in a time of crisis right now or whether you are preparing and bracing for a crisis storm, conserve your resources, but do not hoard them. The secret to thriving in times of crisis is to effectively manage the resources you have, starting with the most important ones. Find out what your fruit is and multiply it. Ask God to help you do it. Rely on His guidance and His strength all day long, every day of your life. Then when a crisis hits, you will be able to manage that too, with the strength that God supplies.

If, in the course of fulfilling your Kingdom responsibilities, you discover that you have strayed somewhat, get back on the path by repenting and going back to where you strayed, so you can resume making progress. If you accumulate too much stuff or too many extra responsibilities and you have to off-load something, do it as fast as you can. If you have to change your tactics, change quickly.

You will have to work hard, so just do it. Do not be lazy. Keep pressing forward.

Do not make your personal comfort your primary goal. Yes, you will get tired. You will hurt sometimes. You will suffer physical, emotional, and spiritual storms. Some of your toil and sweat is not crisis-grade toil and sweat; it is just the normal level for your life. Sometimes, though, you will hit a crisis time, and so will the people around you.

A crisis is always uncomfortable, but do not worry about the discomfort. You will be all right. God is still in charge. His words to Adam apply to you, right in the middle of your current crisis: Be fruitful. Multiply. Subdue the earth. Just keep doing it, even if your tactics have to change because of your circumstances.

Get beyond managing your crisis. Start thriving, right in the midst of it! Soon, your crisis will be history, and you will enter into a time of new abundance.

CHAPTER 8

Job Crisis: Discovering
Your Work Beyond Your Job

*The test of our religion is whether it fits us to
meet emergencies. A man has no more character
than he can command in a time of crisis.*
— *Ralph W. Sockman*

In the previous chapters, I have been explaining about
how our God-given purpose on this earth is *management,* and how effective management is expressed through
our *work.* Just as God set Adam to work tilling the soil in the
Garden, so He sets us to work in many different ways.

However, it is altogether too easy to confuse your divinely
ordained work with your income-producing job or career. We
call our jobs our "work." We say, "I'm going to work now," or
"I'll do that after work." And when we lose our jobs, which

usually means entering into a time of personal crisis, we say, "I am out of work."

Have you lost your job recently? Are you out of work right now? I want to assure you that no, you're not "out of work." In this chapter, I will help you tell the difference between your job and your work.

Jobs Versus Work

Your *job* is what you were trained to do. You may have gone to school to learn your job. On your job, you have certain duties, and you get paid for doing them. But as you well know, your employer can always find somebody else who has been trained to do that particular job, or your boss can decide that a person is no longer needed to do that job. All too easily, you can be replaced, laid off, or fired. Sometimes the company you work for will fail and close its doors, causing you and all of your fellow employees to lose your jobs.

But your *work* is different. Your work is what you were born to do. No kind of educational system can teach you your true work because it is your life purpose, and it is revealed by your God-given gifts. No employer on earth can take that away from you. Nobody can fire you from that. They can lay you off from a job, but they cannot lay you off from being yourself. When you leave a job, you take your work, which is your innate purpose, with you. Wherever you land, you can plant your giftedness so that it can start to grow again. You are much more than your job.

We all need to think about our jobs, and we need to put effort into satisfying the requirements of our jobs. But we also need to think about our true work, our purpose in life, our God-given assignment. Whether you are currently job-hunting or happily employed, you should spend just as much time trying to find your*self* as you spend trying to find a job or satisfy the people you work for. Shift your thinking. If you can find your*self*, you will gain a new perspective on what you were created to do on this earth.

You were not created to punch a time clock. That's just what you may happen to be doing at the beginning and end of your workdays. You were created to contribute to the great bringing-in of the Kingdom of God. The King created you, and the King called you. He gave you special gifts that match with His purpose for your life. He wants you to discover that purpose so that you can fulfill it.

Wherever You May Go, Whatever You May Have

Fulfilling your God-given purpose can happen wherever you go. By God's grace, you can do your *work* even if you are "out of work" at the moment. God likes to move people around. He makes sure that He has representatives in many places, and that includes as many workplaces and job categories as possible, including the "unemployed" category. Your work is ongoing, throughout your life on this planet.

Your job is only your career. It is temporary. You can lose it. Your whole career can collapse. You can also have more than one career in your lifetime. But your work is your life assignment. You cannot lose that. Yes, you can let it languish, unexplored and untried, but you cannot lose the assignment you were born with. You cannot be deprived of your innate gifts and life purpose even if you are deprived of a paying job for a long time.

Whatever you were born with, you were born with. It will not matter how many times you move around; you will still have what you were born with. It will not matter if you are mistreated and run out of town, you will still carry what you were born with. It will not wear out, and it will not disappear. Nobody can take your life assignment away from you. It is like this: you can chase a bird from your porch, but you cannot take away its ability to fly.

In terms of careers and other "things," every single individual who has ever been born came into this world without a single thing. You were not born with a flat-screen TV (in case you didn't know that). You were born without a stitch of clothing on. You did not have an electric kettle when you were born. (You were not even born with three rocks, some kindling, and a dirty pot.) If God seems to have been stripping you of everything lately—of not just your job but also of your possessions and your whole lifestyle—maybe He is stripping you down so that you can find out who you really are.

What were you born with? What were you created to accomplish? What *work* does He have for you to do? He will resupply you with the right "things" and resources so you can step into your life's work.

You qualified for your job because you had picked up certain skills. You may have been born with a certain aptitude, but you had to develop the skills that build on the aptitude. You may be very good at what you do for a living. You may have had the same job for many years, and it may seem to be very stable. However, in an economic crisis, your particular skill may become completely useless. Crises have no respect for how long you have been working.

A simple example: if you are a carpenter—and a good one—but construction is down because of a recession, you simply cannot find anybody who will hire you. So your well-developed skill is useless. You never thought it would happen, but it has happened. Unexpectedly, you need to "re-tool," as they say, reinventing yourself as something other than a carpenter, at least for now. Or maybe you are a bartender in a resort hotel. The Bahamas is loaded with hotels and bars, and you would think that even if you lose your job for some reason, you could get the same kind of job in another establishment. Well, not if your hotel shuts down and none of the other hotels are hiring. All of a sudden, you need to learn to tend something else.

Perhaps you think this does not apply to you because you are retired. You no longer have to worry about finding and keeping a job. While it is true that you have retired from your job, it is not true that you have retired from your work. You can retire from your job, but you cannot retire from your work because you were born to carry it out, and your assignment will take a lifetime to accomplish. You cannot retire from your work because you cannot retire from yourself. You have never heard of a bird retiring from flying, have you?

Never Confuse Your Work With Your Job

You can lose many jobs in your life. Maybe you already have lost many jobs, and you are not too sure about the one you have right now. You cannot let your job become your life because if you lose your job, you lose your purpose in life. You do not want to risk that outcome.

When you start looking at your *work*, what you were born to do, you will find your true purpose. Let's say your job is to be a photographer. People say you are a "gifted photographer." Does that mean that photography is your God-given gift and therefore your true work? Not exactly. However, having an eye for beauty and aesthetics is. Your gift of being able to perceive beauty and transmit it to others supports your job, which is being a photographer. Your gift may also be expressed in other ways.

Are you a nurse? Does that mean that nursing is your gift? Well, it is your job to be a nurse, but underneath your job skills, you may find your gifts of compassion and service. What if you had never become a nurse, but rather had spent all of your life being a hard-working parent and grandparent? You could have expressed that same gifting. Your work is your loving, compassionate service to other people.

The bottom line is this: never confuse your work with your job. Pay attention to this difference, so that you can hone in on your real work, whether or not it happens in the context of your job environment. Jobs are temporary. Work is permanent.

Here, in list format, is a summary of what I have just presented above:

1. Your job is what you were trained to do, but your work is what you were born to do.
2. Your job is your career, but your work is your life assignment.
3. Your job is your skill, but your work is your gift.
4. You can be fired from your job, but you can never be fired from your work.
5. You can retire from your job, but you can never retire from your work.
6. Jobs are temporary. Work is permanent.

Work *Plus* Job

All that being said, it is not as if jobs and work are unrelated. In fact, many times your job prepares you for your work. I have had many jobs in my life, and every one of those jobs is still paying off in my life right now. You should be using every one of your jobs to help refine your gift. Then when you get released from a job, you still have a valuable gift to carry with you.

Do you remember how Moses was fired from his job? Moses used to be a prince. He was a top executive in Egypt. He grew up in the pharaoh's household, so you would think that God would have wanted Him to stay in that job. However, he got fired, and he became a fugitive. He ended up in the Midian desert. He got married, and he decided to take the job of tending his father-in-law's sheep. This was a very different job in a very different place. (See the second and third chapters of the Book of Exodus to review the whole story.)

How did that job prepare Moses for his true work? It prepared him by teaching him how to operate as a shepherd, and those are exactly the skills he was going to need in order to lead the people of Israel across the wilderness to the Promised Land. God knew, from Moses' birth, that his work was to do that. The only difference was that instead of taking sheep through the desert, he would take people through the desert. For years and years, while he was herding his father-in-law's sheep, Moses learned how to organize and lead reluctant followers, how to deal with the desert environment, how to find the water and the food, and so forth. His job prepared him for his real work, which was leading the people of Israel to a God-ordained land where they could be free from slavery.

Sometimes your work creates your job. That is how I feel about my work and job. My work is to teach and provide leadership and spread the Kingdom of God. When I was about 14 years old, I discovered my gift. I discovered my value in the Kingdom, so I came into my adult life already knowing, "Life, you need me. I was born to make a difference." I have been developing an international ministry ever since the 1980s. My gift and my job enrich and enhance each other.

In the Old Testament, we see how Joseph's gift created his job. The pharaoh asked Joseph a question: "How is it possible for you to interpret dreams?" Joseph answered that it was a gift that God had given him. (See Genesis 41.) Pharaoh was so grateful for this gift of interpreting dreams with wisdom, that he put Joseph in charge of the whole country. That is a very clear example of somebody getting a job purely because of his God-given gift.

Your work protects you from your job. What I mean is that when you discover your gift from God, whatever it is, you become eternally valuable. You now have a recession-proof job—fulfilling your purpose. Nobody can take it away from you. You have a gift, and it was given to you for the sake of humanity. You are eternally valuable. In terms of your perspective, God wants you to stop depending on your job and start tapping into your gift.

There is no future in any job. The future is in the one who holds your job (you). Carry your gift with you. Nobody can take your gift away from you.

Your future is in your work. Think beyond your job.

The Power of Work

You were not born just to make a living. You were born to make a difference in the world. The world needs you. Your neighbor needs you—and you need your neighbor. You may not know what your purpose is yet, but it is in there. God knows. He wants to show you.

Your life purpose may seem to be in seed form right now, but if you remember what we talked about in Chapter 6, you will realize that your work is your seed. Your work is your seed, and your seed is your work. As you plant your gift, you grow in your work. You multiply it. A tiny seed carries within it the capacity to become a mighty fruit-bearing tree.

I met a woman in Mount Airy, Pennsylvania, when I was speaking at a conference. She was a housekeeper at the hotel, but she sat in on my sessions. She listened when I taught about finding your gift and living out your potential. On the next-to-the-last day, she sought me out and spoke to me. She said, "You touched my gift today."

The next day, she came, and she brought me some cookies she had baked. She just gave them to me. She said, "This is my gift." I took them back to my hotel room and bit into a cookie. I tell you, I had an *experience*. I had to take my shoes off and wiggle my toes! I don't know what that woman put into that cookie, but whatever it is, I never knew it existed on the earth. I went back to the evening session, and I found her.

I said to her, "Madam, this *is* your gift. You are not really a hotel worker, making beds. You are a cookie maker. You need to take this gift and start serving with it." I gave her instructions to start baking those cookies and giving them away free to all of her family and friends—like drugs ("get the first one free")— just to see what would happen.

I went back to Mount Airy one year later, to the day. There were a lot of people there, but one particular woman stood out. She was dressed in a beautiful suit, and she looked like a million dollars. I didn't even recognize her, but it was that same woman. She said, "Do you remember me? I am the woman from last year. I am the cookie lady."

I said, "Oh, my goodness! Do you have any more cookies?" She gave me a beautiful bag with a beautiful name on it, and inside were some of those cookies, packed in cellophane with a beautiful label on them. She told me her story.

"When you left, I started baking my cookies and giving them away. The cookies started to be in demand. My family started ordering batches of cookies for their parties and so did the folks who worked in the hotel. I started making hundreds of cookies every week.

"Now I have a cookie factory. I employ over a hundred people. Stores in the city started buying the cookies. The bookstores even started buying them. I am not a hotel maid anymore."

I gave her a kiss, took the bag, and went back to my hotel room. I couldn't wait to get to the cookies. When I opened the bag, I found a sealed white envelope. I tore it open. It was $10,000 with a little thank-you note. She said, "Thank you for tapping into my cookie gift."

I think we need more "cookie ladies." What a good testimony to the power of tapping into your gift.

Kingdom Keys for Insulating Yourself From a Job Crisis

This book is about overcoming every crisis. It tells you how to take on the perspective of the Kingdom of God so that you cannot only overcome every crisis in your own life, but you can also grow into a new level of maturity.

A job crisis absolutely fits the definition of a crisis, which is as follows:

> A crisis is an event, a circumstance, or a situation that affects you or your environment, over which you have no direct control or responsibility.

In a job crisis, you cannot alter the situation. One way or the other, you have lost your job, and you cannot have it back. Most of the time, it takes you by surprise. One day, you go to work as usual. It is your job, right? Your boss calls you in, and you find out that you now no longer have a job. Even if you could see it coming, it is still a shock. You can never quite prepare for losing your job.

You have no control over the outcome of that meeting with your boss. You cannot beg to get your job back. Even if you did, your employer's mind is made up. You simply cannot work there anymore.

You *do* have control, however, over your thoughts and your perception. You are always able to control what goes on in your mind. You can evaluate the circumstance and come up with a resolution about it. You can adopt a Kingdom mindset about your situation. A Kingdom mindset will insulate you from the job crisis at hand.

A Kingdom mindset will help you look for the work beyond your job. With a Kingdom mindset, you will be able to make good decisions about what to do next. You will not panic. You will not become depressed.

With a Kingdom mindset, you will be able to look at the whole picture. Even if hundreds of other people are being laid off from their jobs, even if the whole economy is tanking, you will have a firm grip on God because you will know that He has a firm grip on you. You will know that He put you here for a reason, and it was not so that you could stand in an unemployment line. You will know that this is just temporary. Your permanence is with God, and He is a Rock that cannot be shaken. Secure in Him, you will be able to focus on your true work, which is beyond your job.

A Nation in Depression

If you have a Kingdom mindset, you will not have to go into a depression even if your whole nation goes into an economic depression. An economic depression causes a mass depression in the citizens of a nation. It makes the psyche of a nation turn into a negative spirit. It is worse than a recession, which simply reflects the impact of events on the economy.

An economic depression causes desperation. In a depression, people lose hope. They feel as if they have no control over events that are much bigger than they are. They begin to despair. Their livelihood has been taken away. Their life gets taken over by some bank or company that repossesses their material goods. People may hit bottom. They may consider suicide as an option.

One crisis piles on top of another. Domestic violence, divorce, abandonment, abuse, and crime increase. People begin to hurt one another because they are so frustrated and hopeless about not having any control over their situations. People try to earn money in illegal and illicit ways. A major crisis has a ripple effect.

People become afraid. They lock their doors and guard what they have left. They feel threatened. They defend themselves, sometimes with violence.

People feel helpless in the face of a crisis of this proportion. They feel like they have been caught in a hurricane or a tornado. What can they do now? It is beyond their control. They did not start it. They did not create it. A huge storm has come upon them, and they cannot stop it. Their world is spinning out of control.

The Power of Response

You do not have to become sucked into the storm. Even if your whole nation is in a crisis and there is nothing you can do about your circumstances, you have one thing left: the power of your response. You can choose to view the situation from God's perspective. You can hang on to Him, knowing that He will help you figure out what to do.

You are always in control of one thing: your mind. You are always in control of your perception of what is happening. While you cannot control a hurricane or tornado or the crisis that is swirling around you, you can control how you think about it.

Your perception is all-important. Whatever you perceive a thing to be determines how you react to it. You have heard the statement many times, "Don't make a mountain out of a molehill." It is all a matter of perception.

We live more out of what we think about our circumstances than we do out of the circumstances themselves. It's not what happens to you that matters; it's what you do about what happens that matters. And what you do about it depends on what you think about it.

In other words, your response is more important than your experience. That is why it is so important to make sure that your response as an individual is formed by a Kingdom mindset. If enough individuals have a Kingdom mindset, the larger community, even the nation, can be affected.

You already know the situation. The storm has arrived, and it is doing damage as you watch. Doing nothing is not an option. You cannot just sit down and wait for this crisis to pass. If you have just lost your job, you need to find another source of income. Even if the whole nation is in the throes of an economic depression, you need to find a way to feed your family.

Don't wait for a handout. Don't wait for somebody to bring you the solution. Don't sit in your house praying, expecting God to drop a care package through the roof. You had better get out there and start doing something. If you are a part of the Kingdom of God, you have got to be proactive. Stop being a consumer…start being a *pre*sumer. Stop being a victim, and start being the one who creates the victories.

Doing nothing is not an option. Therefore, you have got to respond, and you have got to do it effectively.

The Power of Thoughts and Words

Because the only thing you can be in control of in a crisis is your own thoughts, you need to pay attention to them. Sometimes it is like harnessing bucking horses to take charge of your thoughts, but that does not mean you should not do it. You can control your perception of the crisis situation, and you must do it if you expect to overcome the crisis.

Controlled perception is not a denial of reality but the control of one's response to reality. Whatever you call a thing, whatever you name it, that is what it is going to become to you. Your response to a thing is controlled and determined by whatever that thing is to you.

If you call your new shoes "shoes," but I call them "dead cows," we have given them names that are quite different. My response may be meant as an insult. It is negative. It arouses a degree of shock. It might imply that I would never wear such things on my feet. So much can come from such simple words.

The story of Lazarus in the Bible illustrates the power of perception (see chapters 11 and 12 of the Gospel of John). Lazarus' illness was a crisis, not only for Lazarus himself, but also for his sisters and his friends.

Jesus was one of Lazarus' best friends, and He was off somewhere in the countryside with His disciples when Lazarus fell ill. Martha and Mary, Lazarus' sisters, sent a series of messages to Jesus. When we read the story, we find that Jesus' words kept on contradicting their messages.

When they said, "Lazarus is sick," Jesus responded, "The sickness is not unto death."

When they said, "Lazarus has gotten worse," Jesus responded, "He will be OK."

When they sent a message that said, "Lazarus is sick unto death," Jesus responded, "Don't worry; he is going to be all right."

When they sent a last message that said, "Lazarus has died," Jesus responded, "He is not dead; he has just fallen asleep."

Was Jesus out of touch with reality? On the contrary, He was expressing the reality of the situation better than anybody could have realized. If you say Lazarus is dead, you are saying that it is over, that nobody will be able to wake him up. But if you say he is "sleeping," you have altered the response to the situation. Now it makes sense to say, "So let's go wake him up."

The same kind of thing can apply to you if you have just lost your job. If you think of yourself as "unemployed," and by that you imply that you are a hopeless failure who cannot handle life, your response will be to give up. But if you are more like those who see *crisis* as a word that has "opportunity" tucked into it, you will think of yourself as "not yet employed"—in other words, your response will be to seek the next opportunity.

When I talk about controlling your perception and response, I am not suggesting that you deny reality. You just don't let circumstances take advantage of you. You look for the deeper reality that is hidden by the circumstances.

I am not walking around saying that there is not really an economic crisis and that people are not really losing jobs and homes. I'm not saying that something bad is really good. I am saying that my interpretation of the facts is different. I come from a different culture—a Kingdom culture. In the culture of the Kingdom of Heaven, we can say, "So let's go wake it up."

The Power of Words

Do not underestimate the power of words. You will find that the Book of Proverbs is a rich source for God's Word about words. Consider this proverb, for example: "The tongue has the power of life and death, and those who love it will eat its fruit" (Prov. 18:21). Here is how The Message renders it: "Words kill, words give life; they're either poison or fruit—you choose" (Prov. 18:21 TM).

In other words, even if everything is falling apart, the thing that has the most power over life and death is the human tongue—words. If you say, "Oh, Lord, how am I going to make it to the end of the month?" you will eat the fruit of that. You have just spoken words of death to your hope and faith. You can choose words of life instead: "Oh, Lord, I know You are going to help me make it to the end of the month."

Death and life are not in the circumstances or in the environment. They are not in the events or in the crisis. Death and life are in what you say about the situation.

Another proverb goes like this: "With his mouth the godless destroys his neighbor, but through knowledge the righteous escape" (Prov. 11:9). Take that truth and apply it to job losses. Don't go around saying to your neighbors, "Boy, everybody is getting laid off. You had better be careful because no way are you going to escape. You are going to get laid off, too. This is going to be rough on everybody. You may not survive this downturn. You may lose your house, your car, the dog, and the CD player...." Instead of that, tell your neighbor, "I know you are going to come through this shining. When it's over, you are going to be stronger than you are right now. Your family is going to be all right. You are going to be resourceful and courageous. You are going to prosper." Tell your neighbor, "There's life after the test, so I'll see you on the other side of the test!"

Your words have a lot of power. The writer of Proverbs goes on to say:

Through the blessing of the upright a city is exalted,
but by the mouth of the wicked it is destroyed.

A man who lacks judgment derides his neighbor,
but a man of understanding holds his tongue
(Proverbs 11:11-12).

You are one of the "righteous" from Proverbs 11:9. You are one of the "upright" from Proverbs 11:11, and you are a citizen of the Kingdom of Heaven. That means that you have some knowledge that ordinary earth-citizens do not have. In this time of crisis, it is time for you to speak some of that godly knowledge into the situation. Your Savior has overcome the world, and surely you will overcome this crisis.

Adjust your perspective…you are from the Kingdom of Heaven. You happen to be living on the earth at the moment, but you are governed by a King who rules in your heart, so you can let His perception overrule any outsider's perception.

You can be like all of those people in the Bible who were promoted—which, in case you have not noticed, seemed to happen after a crisis, every time. Daniel used to be an under-secretary in the government. After he came up out of the lions' den, the king promoted him to satrap, which is like being deputy prime minister. Joseph was just a slave in prison, working as the assistant to the jailer. After he came out of prison to interpret the pharaoh's dream, the pharaoh promoted him to second-in-command over the nation.

Have you been asking God for promotion? This crisis you are in right now may be God's program for the answer to your prayer. Say yes to it. Don't get upset about it. Don't lose your peace or your faith in the King. Ask Him for help in thinking about it. Use faith-filled words when you talk about it.

Take hold of statements from the Bible. The Bible says, "…Let the weak say, 'I am strong'" (Joel 3:10 NKJV). It doesn't say that the weak person has to *feel* strong. God just tells the weak person to declare in a crisis, "I *am* strong."

A Crisis Is the Source of Creativity

A crisis is simply a change in the environment that demands a new, unscheduled response. This is one of the reasons that I say that a crisis is the source of creativity.

When you see what is happening, it demands a response from you. To a large extent, you can control your thoughts, perceptions, and responses. If you adopt a Kingdom mindset about the crisis, your mind will not be paralyzed by fear. Often, you will find that you can come up with something totally new. You will think of strategies and further responses that nobody else is thinking of.

Let's look at one case in point: the apostle Paul. Here is one of his statements from his letter to the Romans: "We know that in all things God works for the good of those who love Him, who have been called according to His purpose" (Rom. 8:28). How can you disappoint a man with that perspective? He believes—and he wants us to believe—that God works *all* things for the good of those who love Him, even the most horrendous things. Paul was acquainted with crises. He lost count of the number of times he was chased out of town, banished, shipwrecked, stoned, and so forth. And yet he was firm in his perception that God works every single circumstance for his good.

Was this true because Paul was an apostle, a guy who was extra-holy and extra-good? No, it was because he loved God, and he knew that God had called him according to His purpose, that's all. Paul had a Kingdom mindset.

Paul knew that he had been sent to help infiltrate the earth's culture with the Kingdom culture. The One who sent him is in control of everything, including the latest crisis. So why should he not believe that God would work out His plan regardless of every small-to-Him crisis?

Paul knew that he only needed to be open to God's creative suggestions for how to handle the crisis. The townspeople want to kill you? Maybe you could escape over the city wall in a basket (see Acts 9:23-25). Your enemies want to put you into a fiery furnace? Maybe God will make you inflammable like Shadrach, Meshach, and Abednego (see Dan. 3). You and your people are scheduled for annihilation? Maybe God will give you amazing courage and insightful strategies as He did for Esther (see the Book of Esther).

If you are in the Kingdom of God, even crucifixion turns into victory. Let yourself be permeated with that Kingdom way of looking at your crisis. It will help you overcome.

Up and Down

Recently my wife and I were in Orlando, Florida, and we had dinner in the home of a friend who lives in one of those upper-class gated communities. The smallest house in the community was worth half a million dollars, and they went up in value to about two million dollars.

To my surprise, my friend told me that their gated community had not been insulated from the present economic crisis. In fact, right and left, people were losing their homes to foreclosure. He said, "For many of them, their stock market portfolio collapsed in one day, and they went from being millionaires to being paupers."

I said, "That can't be true."

So after dinner he took me on a neighborhood tour, and we counted the "For Sale" signs: one, two, three, four.... The houses were empty. The people had just walked out. Their assets had vanished.

How do you explain to your five-year-old child why you just moved from a $2-million mansion to an apartment? That is a crisis just as much as any other crisis.

All of us are on escalators in life. Some are going up, and some are going down. You are always moving. No one is stationary. There is no true stability in your circumstances, none at all. Even if you have a Ph.D. and tenure and you are a member of a union, you can still lose that job. Even if you have millions of dollars, you can still lose it easily.

You should keep one eye on the escalators, but always keep your other eye on God. Transfer your expectations from external dependency to an internal revelation of who you are as a citizen of God's Kingdom. Keep moving, and keep growing. You are on the escalator to Heaven!

CHAPTER 9

Kingdom Deployment

Without the strength to endure the crisis, one will not see the opportunity within. It is within the process of endurance that opportunity reveals itself.
—Chin-Ning Chu

Asuccessful career should *not* be your goal in life, or in mine. More than a good job, our goal in life should be successful deployment. What do I mean by that? Let's look at *deployment* versus *employment*—two words that are related but not the same.

As a citizen of the Kingdom of Heaven, your employment—your job, the place where you earn a paycheck—gives you an opportunity to serve and to use the gift God has given you in the context of a corporate group. Your actual place of employment may be large or small. Your particular job description may or may not involve reaching out beyond that specific location. In most cases, your influence will be relatively limited.

However, to be *deployed* as a citizen of God's Kingdom means that you have discovered what your gifts are and you are able to "serve your gift" to your entire generation. You are serving in the context of a much larger group of people and for a much larger "organization," the Kingdom of Heaven. As you work and serve, you are doing far more than earning a paycheck and doing your little part to keep the local economy moving. Your working and your serving come from your relationship with the King, and you are obeying His wishes. You are able to do your work because you can draw on the energy and other resources that He supplies.

Deployment is the giving of your natural giftedness to the world around you. When you get deployed, you serve up your gift to the world. Deployed as a citizen-soldier of the Kingdom, you can be sure that the results of your labor will have eternal significance. Your work matters, and the fruit of your work remains. Here is what Jesus said about Kingdom deployment:

Remain in Me, and I will remain in you. No branch can bear fruit by itself; it must remain in the vine. Neither can you bear fruit unless you remain in Me.

I am the vine; you are the branches. If a man remains in Me and I in him, he will bear much fruit; apart from Me you can do nothing (John 15:4-5).

A person who has been deployed has come into a position and is ready for use, much like a soldier who is positioned in battle formation alongside other soldiers. That person's gifts will be best utilized in that position, and that person has been prepared beforehand for deployment.

Just as somebody who is employed has an employer, so somebody who gets deployed has a "deployer." In your case, the one who deploys you is God Himself. He is the one who positions you for service and usefulness. In addition, He is the one who trains you before deploying you.

Created to Serve, Destined for Greatness

You were created to be deployed. You were created to serve the world around you with Kingdom compassion and Kingdom energy. The Kingdom of God is characterized by a culture of servanthood, and Jesus is the foremost example of this kind of servanthood. He both modeled it and taught it. He explained to His disciples that they should not look for status or high position, and that they should not lord it over other people, but rather serve others:

Jesus called them together and said, "You know that the rulers of the Gentiles lord it over them, and their high officials exercise authority over them. Not so with you. Instead, whoever wants to become great among you must be your servant, and whoever wants to be first must be your slave—just as the Son of Man did not come to be served, but to serve, and to give His life as a ransom for many" (Matthew 20:25-28).

In Jesus' words, "Whoever wants to become great among you must be your servant, and whoever wants to be first must be your slave." Someone who is "first" is the first one whom people call on when they have a need. A person who is "great" may or may not hold a political office or some worldly leadership position, but that person is seen as hardworking and dependable.

Are people always asking you for help? If so, you should take it as a good sign that you are reflecting the character of your King. If not, it may be time to take a close look at your attitude, your work habits, and your motivations. Maybe people can tell that you are not inclined to serve and that, in fact, you are rather self-focused. Maybe they can tell that instead of reaching out to others, you tend to hold back or even to demand services from them.

What is another way that you can be sure that you are reflecting the King's character and that you have a true heart of service? Look at your attitude toward work. Do you shoulder your share of the work without murmuring or complaining? If so, then you have probably already been deployed in the service of the King. You probably already know that being a servant is not a bad thing. Far from indicating that you are merely subservient, finding joy in your work indicates that you have found your God-given gift (or gifts) and that you are willing to share what He has given you with the world around you.

And that alone is enough to make you "great" in the Kingdom of God.

The Power of Your Gifts

The Kingdom of God operates in a most unique way. It is the only kingdom anywhere that designates every single citizen as a king in his or her own right. You are a king, and I am a king. The person who sat next to you at last week's worship service is a king, too.

This is a high privilege and an honor. Being a king also carries with it a built-in expectation that you and I will spend all of the days of our lives serving. We are servant kings. We work our way up the Kingdom management ladder by working our way down in lowly service. We are kings who serve the world with our God-given gifts.

In this Kingdom, our kingship reflects our divine King's management mandate. We have been created to be kings over specific arenas. We have been granted particular resources over which we are supposed to exercise Kingdom authority. We do not hold Kingdom authority over our fellow Kingdom citizens, but rather over a wide range of resources.

The resources over which we exercise Kingdom authority are determined by our specific areas of gifting. We have been deployed into the world to exercise this authority with Kingdom wisdom, with Kingdom influence, and (as a result) with Kingdom greatness. As the proverb states, "A gift opens the way for the giver and ushers him into the presence of the great" (Prov. 18:16).

This is why the Lord Jesus is referred to as the King of kings and the Lord of lords. Not only is He the ruler of worldly rulers, He is also the ruler of the hundreds of thousands of people like you and me, believers who are citizen-kings in His Kingdom. He is able and willing to equip each one of us for our specific roles and also to sustain us in them.

Although you and I will be required to serve humbly and to work hard under our King, we are guaranteed one glorious reward: an eternal life filled with His all-rewarding presence. In the midst of our lives of service, we will find that every day is a good day. It will not matter what kinds of crises swirl around us. The Kingdom of God is the most stable entity of all—and you and I are a part of it.

Leadership and Work

As a king in the Kingdom of God, you are a leader and a servant at the same time; you are a servant-leader. Your King loves you, and it is His delight to allow you to share in His rulership over the earth.

But being a king in the Kingdom does not mean that you are going to get a free ride. To step into your role, you must agree to the idea that you will be required to *work*. In fact, being deployed as part of the Kingdom workforce means that you will be required to work very hard. However, you will not mind working hard for your King and this Kingdom of His because you will find so much fulfillment in using the gifts He has given you. As you work, you will find encouragement in becoming fruitful and productive. You will find particular joy in receiving the commendation, "Well done," from your King.

Your work in the Kingdom is so different from your work in your place of employment. Although much of your Kingdom deployment can and will infiltrate your earthly employment, the pay scale and the rewards are quite different. In your place of employment, you are looking for your paycheck. You may or may not enjoy what you are doing on the job. If your job happens to employ your gifts and you like it, so much the better. In your place of *de*ployment, the work itself is your reward. You go forth into each day to work in the section of the "garden" to which He has assigned you. As His co-worker, you have a share in His creativity.

In your Kingdom assignment, you express a portion of His lordship. You are like a deputy king, laboring and leading the way, bringing life to what is dead and light to what is dark. You are co-laboring with Him.

When God created the earth and all that is in it, He worked. He *labored*, in the sense of working as well as in the sense of giving birth. He labored to bring forth the wonders that were hidden inside Him.

Then when He created Adam and Eve and dignified them with the role of becoming co-laborers with Him, managing all that He had created, He released them to do the same thing—to work to bring forth the wonders that were hidden inside themselves in the form of giftings. The gifts were, as I have said in earlier chapters, like seeds. Planting and taking care of these seeds is your work and mine. In the process of carrying out our work, we feel fulfilled because we are finding our true purpose.

The Greek word for "work" that is used throughout the New Testament is *ergon*. It has several shades of meaning, one of which is "to become." Through your work, you "become." You fulfill your potential, and you are fulfilled in the process. You manifest yourself as the person God created you to be. You release your God-given gifts, in essence releasing yourself. You push out your gifts like a mother in labor pushes out the child. You "serve yourself out" as you work, releasing your gift in an ongoing way.

Take a look at these sample verses from the New Testament in which this Greek word for work, *ergon*, is used. (I have boldfaced the key words.)

*In the beginning, O Lord, You laid the foundations of the earth, and the heavens are the **work** of Your hands* (Hebrews 1:10).

*For we are God's **workmanship**, created in Christ Jesus to do good **works**, which God prepared in advance for us to do* (Ephesians 2:10).

*But just as He who called you is holy, so be holy in all you do; for it is written: "Be holy, because I am holy." Since you call on a Father who judges each man's **work** impartially, live your lives as strangers here in reverent fear* (1 Peter 1:15-17).

But to each one of us grace has been given as Christ apportioned it. This is why it says:

"When He ascended on high,
He led captives in His train
and gave gifts to men."

*....It was He who gave some to be apostles, some to be prophets, some to be evangelists, and some to be pastors and teachers, to prepare God's people for **works** of service, so that the body of Christ may be built up until we all reach unity in the faith and in the knowledge of the Son of God*

and become mature, attaining to the whole measure of the fullness of Christ (Ephesians 4:7-8; 11-13).

Let us think of ways to motivate one another to acts of love and good works. (Hebrews 10:24 NLT).

And we pray this in order that you may live a life worthy of the Lord and may please Him in every way: bearing fruit in every good **work***, growing in the knowledge of God, being strengthened with all power according to His glorious might so that you may have great endurance and patience, and joyfully giving thanks to the Father, who has qualified you to share in the inheritance of the saints in the kingdom of light (Colossians 1:10-12).*

Being a Solution

As a worker in God's garden on this earth, you were born to solve a problem. You are God's response to a need. You are the fulfillment of one of God's desires. You are the answer to a question God knew would be raised in this particular generation into which you have been born. You have been assigned to this generation, and this generation needs to experience what you will be bringing to it.

In short, *you are necessary!*

Just because your King has deployed so many others into this generation does not reduce your importance to Him or to His Kingdom. His Kingdom is vast. His Kingdom is ever-expanding (see Matt. 13:31-32). Yet, He knows every hair on your head (see Matt. 10:30). He sought you out, like a shepherd who looks for a lost sheep (see Matt. 18:12-14).

He did not choose you and call you to become part of His Kingdom just so that He could collect and tally another soul. If He had chosen you and called you just to help populate Heaven, He would have taken you home right away. Instead, He situated you here, in a particular generation in a particular family that lives in a particular country.

He situated you where you are, and He gave you work to do. He said to you, in essence, just as He said to Adam, "Be fruitful and multiply." He has something very specific for you to do while you live in this earth. Your assignment will have ups and downs. It will have glorious, rewarding times, and it will have difficult, crisis-ridden times. Through it all, as you exercise your kingly co-leadership with Him, you will better understand how important it is to work wholeheartedly, together with your King.

Jobs and Your Work

As I have mentioned already, the paying jobs you have held during your life have been given to you in part to prepare you for your true work. You have given yourself to God, and He is in charge of every aspect of your life, including your working life. He blends and knits everything together; He does not waste a thing. He will not waste your experiences in the working world.

Of course, you will not usually be aware of what He is doing. You are just working. You are just going through your days and weeks, hoping and trusting in Him for the outcome. You are taking the advice of the son of David: "Sow your seed in the morning, and at evening let not your hands be idle, for you do not know which will succeed, whether this or that, or whether both will do equally well" (Eccles. 11:6).

You are like a clay pot with a treasure inside. In fact, that is how the apostle Paul referred to each one of us: "We have this treasure in jars of clay to show that this all-surpassing power is from God and not from us" (2 Cor. 4:7).

Paul went on to talk about how, in spite of our status as God's "treasure-holders," our lives could challenge us severely:

We are hard pressed on every side, but not crushed; perplexed, but not in despair; persecuted, but not abandoned; struck down, but not destroyed. We always carry around in our body the death of Jesus, so that the life of Jesus may also be revealed in our body. For we who are alive are always being given over to death for Jesus' sake, so that His life may be revealed in our mortal body. So then, death is at work in us, but life is at work in you (2 Corinthians 4:8-12).

As we go through the years, working and trusting God, we *will* have times of crisis; it is guaranteed. More often than not, our times of crisis will have something to do with our employment. Given the fact that most of us will spend most of our waking hours involved in some form of employment, it is inevitable that a number of the crises in our lives will happen in the context of our jobs.

Does this help you to see your employment from God's perspective? He is using it to get you prepared for your real work, and that includes the hardest moments on the job. If, whether you are employed or unemployed, you maintain your hold on His life every single day, you will continue to be a life-bringer wherever you go. And that is your real work—nurturing the life of the Kingdom in your little corner of the world. Moreover, you will discover true fulfillment when your *job* becomes your *work*, when His life flows through every feature of your day-to-day reality.

Living by Faith

When God created human beings, He designed them to live a Kingdom life. Before long, Adam and Eve learned that they would have to live their lives by faith because the easygoing relationship they had earlier enjoyed with God had been disrupted by their sin.

Sin did not alter God's original intention, however. By His original design, human beings were meant to keep eternity in their hearts. Now they would no longer be able to see clearly, but they could hold on to God anyway.

After Jesus came to Earth and was born, lived, died, and rose again, living by faith became a little easier because He sent His Holy Spirit to each one of the people who believed in Him. Now this life of faith, with all of its ups and downs, made more sense. Now each one of us could ask a Counselor to explain things to us (see John 14:26). Although believers encountered just as many crises as ever, and maybe more, the work of the Kingdom was not blocked by any crisis.

The disciples—and that includes you and me—could now maintain a better focus, thanks to the Holy Spirit, and God's Kingdom could advance. With a little more Heaven in our hearts, we could weather the storms better. In the words of the apostle Paul (whose work for the Kingdom entailed one crisis after another):

We know that when these bodies of ours are taken down like tents and folded away, they will be replaced by resurrection bodies in heaven—God-made, not handmade—and we'll never have to relocate our "tents" again. Sometimes we can hardly wait to move—and so we cry out in frustration. Compared to what's coming, living conditions around here seem like a stopover in an unfurnished shack, and we're tired of it! We've been given a glimpse of the real thing, our true home, our resurrection bodies! The Spirit of God whets our appetite by giving us a taste of what's ahead. He puts a little of heaven in our hearts so that we'll never settle for less.

That's why we live with such good cheer. You won't see us drooping our heads or dragging our feet! Cramped conditions here don't get us down. They only remind us of the spacious living conditions ahead. It's what we trust in but don't yet see that keeps us going. Do you suppose a few ruts in the road or rocks in the path are going to stop us? When the time comes, we'll be plenty ready to exchange exile for homecoming (2 Corinthians 5:1-8 TM).

Thank God for sending His Holy Spirit, so that we can live by faith and not by sight!

The Secret to Kingdom Success

Achieving success in the Kingdom is the same as achieving success at living by faith. Achieving success at living by faith is an ongoing process. Until you personally cross the threshold into Heaven, you will be living by faith and letting the Giver of faith refine you.

You start out as one who has been chosen by the King to dwell in the Kingdom. As you respond to His guidance, you discover your gifting and the work that He wants you to do. Many times, you will move forward to take your next steps into the unknown only because of a crisis of some sort. Therefore, you can be sure that any crisis that the Lord allows in your life is the same as an opportunity for growth. The crises of your life may represent significant, seemingly unsolvable problems, but they are not permanent.

God has given you the ability and the gifts to solve the problems He allows in your life. Do you believe that?

You may be living by faith as much as you know how to do, and yet you remain painfully aware of your shortcomings. Your shortcomings do not bother God. To Him, you possess high value. You are unique, and you are uniquely suited to lay hold of Him in faith, to press on in obedience to whatever He tells you to do, and to overcome the problems that may seem to block your way.

You could even say that overcoming crises—holding tightly to Him in faith—is the secret to success in the Kingdom of God. There are as many paths to success in the Kingdom of God as there are individual people, but every single one of them requires living by faith. Each person needs to have Holy Spirit eyes to see his or her problems as opportunities and then to persevere in solving the problems before being hindered or destroyed by them.

The Gift of Your Seed

The solving of problems, as it turns out, is one definition of a "business." As you discover your gift and discover your assignment, you discover your true business. That is how your Kingdom deployment, which is your giftedness and purpose expressed in your work, can end up overlapping with your employment.

Here is an example that is very close to home—because it is my ministry. In 1980, I decided that we had a problem in the Bahamas. Instead of being a place that was exporting the Kingdom, we seemed to be importing almost everything related to the Kingdom. The Bahamas did not have any church headquarters or any Christian publishing houses or any outreaches to speak of. We traveled by airplanes to Tennessee or to England to report on our work for the Kingdom. It was as if we didn't have any seed of our own, or at least we were not planting the seed that we did have.

Along with a couple of like-minded friends, I decided back in 1980 to plant my seed right here. I decided to become a leader of a Bahamas-based ministry. With God's help, I wanted not to be a copy, but an original.

From my teenage years, I had been aware of areas of gifting that God had put into me. I could see the problems ahead, and I wanted to apply my gifts to solving them. I wanted to found a business that could become so successful that the people in Tennessee and England would come to *us* to report. Bahamas Faith Ministries International (BFMI) was born, with a membership of seven people.

In the nearly 30 years since then, BFMI has become a multi-faceted ministry. It is the largest ministry in the Bahamas, and it has an extensive international outreach. With its subsidiary, the International Third World Leaders Association, BFMI now reaches more than 70 nations with a non-denominational, charismatic message. We are helping to fulfill the Great Commission.

When Jesus was about to ascend to His Father, He charged the disciples to "go and make disciples of all nations, baptizing them in the name of the Father and of the Son and of the Holy Spirit, and teaching them to obey everything I have commanded you…" (Matt. 28:19-20). Here we see that the most important assignment for believers is to "disciple the nations." The word *nations* comes from the Greek word *ethnos*, which means "common groupings." The nations can be further divided into groupings according to discipline. Just as every ethnic grouping has its own language and culture, so too does every discipline, whether it be the world of entertainment, business, education, politics, or medicine. Therefore, Jesus' Great Commission to His disciples more precisely means discipling common groupings of disciplines. In other words, discipling every discipline should be the goal of the Church. This takes wisdom, diplomacy, and skill.

Through the International Leadership Training Institute, BFMI seeks to prepare and equip laborers for the harvest.

Whether the individuals who are trained end up working in the context of a church ministry, a business, or a discipline, they will be able to work effectively as laborers in the harvest. They will be able to do the work of the Kingdom where they have been planted.

Especially because much of our outreach is to Third World countries, we lay a firm foundation of redemption before we get into techniques or academic concerns. We speak to the heart of the issue, which means helping to restore a sense of personal purpose and Kingdom potential and value.

My personal vision is expressed in these four words, "Transforming followers into leaders." Because of my nationality, I have a passion for communicating the message that all people are equals in the sight of God and that every human being has a God-given purpose in life, despite the social disruptions and oppressions of colonialism, the slave trade, and other long-term "crisis" experiences.

You, too, can discover your "seed" and allow the King to deploy you into the harvest field. You may not become the founder of a ministry at all, but your skills, talents, abilities, and characteristics will enable you to fulfill His plan for your life. This can happen in spite of—or even because of—any crisis that presents itself.

Death and Resurrection

Have you ever thought about Jesus' death by crucifixion as a "crisis"? In the context of this book about overcoming crisis, we do not want to ignore it.

At the time of Jesus' death, the band of His believers was not very large, and they certainly were not very influential. As soon as Jesus expired on the cross, they went into hiding. Only a couple of women and one man dared to let themselves be associated with Him by taking care of His burial. Now what would become of them? They had left everything to follow Him, and the One they had followed was dead. This was a crisis of the most monumental proportions. Not only were their very lives in danger from the authorities, they had literally no place to go. What should they do with their lives now? They had left their old lives behind, burned all of their bridges. They did not even know how to earn a living anymore.

The Lord Himself took care of everything. He did not eliminate the dangers or thwart further crises, but He came back in person to set in motion something new. Miracle of miracles, He rose from the dead. Then He set about restoring the shattered lives of those He loved.

After the apostle Peter had disgraced himself by denying the Lord before the crucifixion, the risen Lord paid Him a personal visit. He restored Peter to his original purpose. Do you remember the scene? "Feed my sheep," Jesus told him. (See John 21:15-19.) Immediately, even though Jesus also warned him about impending troubles, Peter was back on track. He and the others would remain faithful from that point forward to follow Jesus unto death.

The same thing happened with Saul, whose name was changed to Paul after his powerful encounter with the risen

Christ on the road to Damascus. He had been a dedicated enemy of Christians, killing them right and left. Instantly, he was transformed into a believer himself, a fearless preacher of the Good News. He described it as discovering his life's purpose: "...It pleased God in His kindness to choose me and call me, even before I was born! ...Then He revealed His Son to me so that I could proclaim the Good News about Jesus to the Gentiles..." (Gal. 1:15-16 NLT). After his experience on the road to Damascus, Paul was *deployed*.

The Challenge

As a nation, the Bahamas still imports 90 percent of what it consumes. Some of this is inevitable because of the limitations of geography and climate. But I believe that our national mentality reflects negative historical experiences. Our expectation is to be junior partners in the world. But as we face the new crises and challenges of the 21st century, I believe that we may be able to lay hold of some more Kingdom truths and principles. If we don't, we will miss out again.

You may know the old saying, "When America sneezes, [name of country] gets pneumonia." Well, I'm grateful for the current crop of crises that are erupting in the United States because I think in the Bahamas we have needed something like this to give us a good national slap. Even though there is a lot of "sneezing" going on, I want us to remain in good health anyway. I want us to stand on our own two feet. In terms of the Kingdom of God, I want us to be deployed to the rest of the world.

Will we accept the challenge? I don't know. But when I look at other island nations—Japan and England for example—or other nations that are very small in size—such as Israel—I can see examples of what I am hoping for. Those nations have also had negative historical experiences, and yet they have succeeded in so many ways.

Every nation is composed of individuals. Unless a large number of people rise to the current challenges, nations can falter. On a personal level, where is a crisis hitting you right now? It does not matter if you live in the Bahamas or elsewhere. What problems have come up that seem almost too big to handle? Have you lost your job, or do you think you might lose it soon? Has your income been reduced? Have your savings been wiped out?

Ask God to forgive you for depending on your job for your significance, and ask Him to help you discover your gift even more. Ask Him to help you tap into the seed that's buried deep down in you. Ask Him to show you what you need to refine and what you need to develop. Ask Him to expand your knowledge of yourself. Ask Him to introduce you to the "you" you never knew, the person on the inside. Ask God to show you your seed, and make a decision to become a tree:

> *What shall we say the kingdom of God is like, or what parable shall we use to describe it? It is like a mustard seed, which is the smallest seed you plant in the ground. Yet when planted, it grows and becomes the largest of all garden plants,*

with such big branches that the birds of the air can perch in its shade (Mark 4:30-32).

The Kingdom of God is within you. That's what Jesus said:

Once, having been asked by the Pharisees when the kingdom of God would come, Jesus replied, "The kingdom of God does not come with your careful observation, nor will people say, 'Here it is,' or 'There it is,' because the kingdom of God is within you" (Luke 17:20-21).

Are you ready for deployment?

CHAPTER 10

Maximizing the Benefits of Crisis

The Chinese use two brush strokes to write the word "crisis." One brush stroke stands for danger; the other for opportunity. In a crisis, be aware of the danger—but recognize the opportunity.—
John F. Kennedy

"Sweet are the uses of adversity," William Shakespeare wrote, and I think that sums up a profound truth.

Adversity is the same as crisis. A crisis, which may seem to be destructive, can turn out to be highly *constructive*—if you know how to maximize its benefits. You can come to see a time of adversity or crisis in a new light because of its many positive features.

The key benefits of any crisis center around the fundamental way a crisis forces us to become innovative and creative. A crisis becomes a driving force. It forces us to come up with inventive solutions, and it makes us willing to take risks. When we are in trouble, we exercise our brains and our faith as we never have before. A crisis is sink-or-swim time.

Remember Peter, walking on the water? (See Matthew 14:24-33.) Peter and the other disciples were crossing the lake at night. Their boat was far offshore, and it was "buffeted by the waves because the wind was against it." That was a crisis already.

Then in the middle of the night, Jesus approached their boat in the darkness. He walked right up to it, striding on top of the waves! They were terrified. They didn't know it was Jesus; they thought it was a ghost. Their crisis had just gotten bigger.

But Jesus identified Himself, changing their terror back to mere fear. Peter, however, took it a step farther—into faith. He challenged the "ghost" who had said He was Jesus. "Lord, if it's You," he said, "tell me to come to You on the water" (Matt. 14:28).

Jesus said, "Come." Peter stepped out of the boat, and was amazed to discover that he could do it. The choppy water was no harder to walk on than a plowed field. There he was, walking right on top of the waves, just as Jesus was! Nobody had ever done that before.

It was a bold, impulsive move for Peter to do that. People can't walk on the surface of a lake. It flies in the face of common sense. The only way it made any sense was as a step of faith. Although Peter took only a few steps before he faltered and began to sink, he had proved the power of faith.

Besides demonstrating the power of faith, Peter had just demonstrated how something brand-new can happen because of a crisis. He certainly would not have done it otherwise.

We Need a Crisis

Peter was a fisherman, remember. He was not afraid of the water itself. On one later occasion, Peter stepped out of a boat and swam to the shore (see John 21:7-8). In that situation, he wanted to reach land faster than he could have done in the boat, so he did the only logical thing: he dove into the water and started swimming. That time, he did not even think of walking on top of the water's surface.

In that earlier, stormy situation, however, Peter was driven to attempt something untried and new. This seems to be the way it always works in a time of emergency. That's why I can say without hesitation: a crisis really does have benefits.

Jon Huntsman, a wealthy businessman and philanthropist, wrote this: "Humans seldom have created anything of lasting value unless they were tired or hurting."[1] If you think about it, you will realize that it is true. It fits with the old saying, "Necessity is the mother of invention." A time of crisis is like an incubator for creativity.

We need times of crisis to jolt us out of our ruts. Without some kind of a crisis, we are not inclined to think hard enough, pray hard enough, or work hard enough to make innovative changes. That's why God allows crises to happen.

The Lord not only allows a crisis, He brings on the crisis. He does it because He knows that trials and problems will always work for our good. Crises will make us grow spiritually, mentally, psychologically, and emotionally. Crises will make us expand. Crises will provide us with plenty of motivation to try something new.

Growth in Crisis

Your maturity and your leadership ability will be tested in a time of crisis. If you think you are mature and stable and strong, a crisis will enable you to see if your level of maturity and stability and strength is as great as you thought it was. If you think you are in charge of your family, you will find out if that is true or not. If you say you are in charge of your business, you and everyone else will find out for sure when a crisis hits. If you are in charge of some level of government, you will find out whether or not you are a good leader. True leadership is tested in crisis.

Leaders get tested in crisis, and leaders grow stronger. Leaders do not develop in good times. They develop and improve only under pressure. Under the pressure of a crisis, your leadership qualities will be sharpened. A crisis places demands on your unreleased potential. When you are under pressure, you will discover areas of your life that you never knew existed. Your ingenuity kicks in. You become industrious. You become a thinker.

Because crisis is the cradle of creativity and because creativity is the same as innovative thinking, you will always find that times of crisis and pressure move you forward into new realms. We never innovate when things are working well. We are forced to innovate when something malfunctions—which is exactly what happens in a time of crisis.

A crisis will reveal your true beliefs and convictions. Have you always said that you believe your God is faithful? Well, what do you say now that you have lost your job and your family home is up for sale? With your true level of faith revealed, you will be forced to see what you can do with it. Will your faith grow? Will you pass the test?

Innovation in Crisis

Abraham passed his test with flying colors when he was faced with a major crisis (see Gen. 22). God created that crisis when He told Abraham to take his only son Isaac onto the mountain to sacrifice him on an altar. Abraham had nothing to go on except his faith. Isaac had been born through a miracle. If God wanted him back, Abraham figured he would have to put aside his fatherly instinct to protect his boy. He obeyed. It was not until Abraham had tied up Isaac with ropes and raised his knife to slit his son's throat that the angel stopped him. The voice of the Lord said, "Now I know that you fear God, because you have not withheld from Me your son, your only son" (Gen. 22:12). Abraham had passed a critical test. God could proceed with His plan to make Abraham's descendents as numerous as the grains of sand on the seashore.

Abraham was completely obedient, but he was also instantly ready to change what he was doing. Dreadful as it seemed, he thought he was going to have to kill his son. But when the angel of the Lord provided a ram instead, Abraham was more than willing to make a substitution. He saw the way out of his dilemma. He seized the animal and sacrificed it instead. Abraham showed a capacity to take a different approach to his crisis situation. By doing so, he demonstrated not only incredible faith, but also how a crisis forces innovation.

So what is innovation? In brief, innovation is the:

- capacity to create new approaches and concepts to deal with old and new challenges.

- perceptivity to see possibilities in the combination of old and new concepts.

- creation, development, and application of untested ways of solving old and new problems.

- capacity to think beyond the known, to defy the norm, and to believe in one's abilities to solve problems.

Innovation does not create new raw materials. All of the raw materials are already created. Innovation recombines them in fresh ways. "There is nothing new under the sun," Ecclesiastes 1:9 says. Everything that we call "new" is a new grouping of old things. The exact combination and the timing of the combination may be new, but the raw materials are not new.

Everything necessary to invent the next new thing is already present in the world. Innovation enables someone to see old things with new eyes and to combine them in new ways for new purposes.

When you go to the store and buy a new pair of shoes, it is an old cowhide that has been cut and stretched and stitched and soled. When you buy a book, the cover and the pages have been made from a plant. When you buy a new suit, it is old sheep wool, "reformatted." When you buy a beautiful new wooden dining room table, it is not as new as you might think because it is really an old tree, worked over and changed into a table. When you buy a "new" car, it is a combination of old metals, petroleum products, and so forth.

You cannot create all-new things any more than you can create new people. (Only God can do that.) But there are always new ways of combining people. You are forced to choose from the people you've got, but you can innovate in the way you combine their strengths.

You are an inventor, which means you are an innovator and a "re-combiner." You are creative, not like God at Creation, making something out of nothing. Rather you are creative at putting some of the already-created stuff together in a new way.

Part of bringing the Kingdom of God to the earth is bringing His creativity to bear on the circumstances that we call crises. With the anointing of the Holy Spirit, the creative juices can really flow. You can begin to see things in a new way and come up with solutions to problems that nobody ever thought of before.

First, though, you have to *have* a problem. When a problem or a crisis is breathing down your neck, you have both the motivation and reason to make something happen. No crisis, no innovative problem solving.

Innovative Thinking

A crisis *requires* innovative thinking. A crisis makes the brain expand beyond its default setting, which is to go to the familiar experiences and solutions. Those old things just won't work anymore. In a crisis, you cannot go "by the book." You must have the capacity to create new approaches to deal with the challenges.

When Moses got to the shore of the Red Sea with the entire people of Israel, he had no idea how to get the people across the water. (See Exodus 14.) Time was short; the Egyptians were already in hot pursuit, raising a cloud of dust in the distance. It was a fear-provoking setup with impassable water in front and certain death behind. Obviously, God (who had just worked a series of miracles to permit the people to depart from their slavery in Egypt and who was still fully in charge of this mass exodus) had allowed it to happen. What was Moses supposed to do?

Moses thought fast. He was desperate. "We need boats—thousands of them." No. No time for that. No boats.

"We must swim." No way. The children can't swim. The old grandmothers can't swim. Most of the people can't swim. It's too far. No. No swimming.

That's all Moses could think of. He only had those two default ideas, and he could see that they were not going to work. Then God broke in with some news: "Tell the Israelites to move on. Raise your staff and stretch out your hand over the sea to divide the water so that the Israelites can go through the sea on dry ground" (Exod. 14:15-16). It didn't make sense to Moses, but neither had the miracles that had happened back in Egypt. So he obeyed.

You know the story. It happened. It worked. The people of Israel were saved, and their pursuers were annihilated. An immense crisis had been turned aside. Old methods may have been useful in other situations, but they would not have worked in this one. Moses had to find a new way of getting the people across the water, and God helped him do it.

What kind of "Red Sea" is in front of you at the moment? Do you feel like Moses did? You need to find a new way to overcome your current crisis. Don't panic. Sit back and consider the situation. You have a brain with 6 trillion cells. You have the Holy Ghost. Get innovative. Let your crisis work for you. Grapple with your crisis and wring out its benefits.

This crisis is exposing some part of your old, familiar pattern that is going to have to come to an end. This crisis is an announcement from God that your old ways of doing things need to be set aside. Your old solutions will not work this time. You are going to need to recombine things.

Of course the process will not be very smooth. After all, it has never been tried before. It is an innovative process, which by definition is risky because of moving into untried and untested territory. Your initiative may attract critics. But if you do not try something new, you are definitely going to go under.

Never Say "Never"

As you overcome your crisis, you have got to believe in yourself almost as much as you believe in God. You have got to believe that He has equipped you to win out over your crisis.

You have got to come to the point where you can say, *"Every* problem has a solution," in spite of the fact that your old solutions are worthless. You know you cannot go home and revert to business as usual. The whole world is slipping away from "business as usual." The whole world is in a crisis, and your personal crisis is just one part of a bigger one. This is part of the reason it seems so daunting.

Nevertheless, do not give up. Do not throw in the towel. Do not quit. Do not take pills. Do not shoot yourself. Every single problem has a solution, and it must be within your grasp or God would not have allowed you to be tested in the first place. Remember:

No test or temptation that comes your way is beyond the course of what others have had to face. All you need to remember is that God will never let you down; He'll never let you be pushed past your limit; He'll always be there to help you come through it (1 Corinthians 10:13 TM).

Your crisis may be big, but God is much bigger. Every problem has a solution, including yours right now. Ask the

Holy Spirit to help you think of the solution. Let your faith grow as you see what He will enable you to do.

Maturity and Crisis

Your present crisis has come to mature you. The end result of a crisis in your own life is increased maturity—if you keep going all the way through it. This is what the apostle James was talking about when he wrote to his fellow believers and told them why they should appreciate their trials and tribulations:

> *Consider it pure joy, my brothers, whenever you face trials of many kinds, because you know that the testing of your faith develops perseverance. Perseverance must finish its work so that you may be mature and complete, not lacking anything* (James 1:2-4).

What does it mean to become mature? A mature person has a well-rounded character. He or she cares about other people, having an expanded capacity for shared joy as well as for shared sorrow, no longer being childishly self-centered.

Mature people are comfortable with themselves the way God made them. They keep on growing as long as they live. A mature person mirrors God's character to others, having experienced the sanctifying work of the Holy Spirit through every trial of life.

A mature person is a full person, not an empty one. A mature person, therefore, has something to give away. He or she is always replacing what has been given away with something more, drawing from a well-supplied storehouse of life experiences—and faith.

In his first letter, the apostle Peter praised the believers to whom he was writing for their maturity of character and faith, which he associated with "all kinds of trials":

> Peter, an apostle of Jesus Christ, to God's elect, strangers in the world, scattered throughout Pontus, Galatia, Cappadocia, Asia and Bithynia, who have been chosen according to the foreknowledge of God the Father, through the sanctifying work of the Spirit, for obedience to Jesus Christ and sprinkling by His blood: Grace and peace be yours in abundance....
>
> In this [salvation] you greatly rejoice, though now for a little while you may have had to suffer grief in all kinds of trials. These have come so that your faith—of greater worth than gold, which perishes even though refined by fire—may be proved genuine and may result in praise, glory and honor when Jesus Christ is revealed (1 Peter 1:1-2;6-7).

One thing is for sure—your times of crisis will work in your favor in terms of your maturity. One of the greatest benefits of facing difficulties is growth in maturity, meaning growth in your ability to reflect godly traits and rock-solid faith.

Earth's Need for Heaven

The people of the earth need the maturity and leadership of the people of God. The whole world is in a critical state, lurching from one crisis to another, filled with fear, anxiety, and confusion. Governments are embroiled in conflict and confusion, bankrupt of solutions for the problems they face. Their economies are disintegrating. Their peace has been shattered by terrorism and war. Only the people of God, who are agents of the Kingdom, can provide what is so desperately needed.

Whether the people of the earth know it or not, what they need is outside help. Not just a little financial aid from a bigger, wealthier country, but help from another realm, from Heaven. The kingdoms of the earth need the Kingdom of Heaven.

Deep inside, people know they cannot solve so many problems by puny human means. Instinctively, they know that they need outside help. That's why they are so captivated with Superman and other superheroes. Superman was born somewhere else, on the fictitious planet Krypton, and he came to earth with superpowers, using his strong moral compass as a guide to help people out of their crises.

I need to point out, however, that Superman is a comic-book hero, and all of the human heroes on earth put together cannot supply enough wisdom and strength to clean up the mess we are in. People are so excited when a strong new leader like Barack Obama comes on the scene because they think he can bring them everything they need. Obama graduated from the same university that the leaders of Wall Street came from. Their collective human wisdom will not be enough. We need God.

Thy Kingdom Come, Thy Will Be Done

Jesus is the true Superhero that we need, and you and I are carrying on His mission of bringing His Kingdom to earth. If our crisis-torn planet can get invaded by the Kingdom of God, this is the greatest benefit that could ever come from all of the desperation.

What is your part? It is simple. Keep living the Kingdom life, and keep praying the Kingdom prayer:

Our Father in heaven,
Hallowed be Your name.
Your kingdom come.
Your will be done
On earth as it is in heaven.
Give us this day our daily bread.
And forgive us our debts,
As we forgive our debtors.
And do not lead us into temptation,
But deliver us from the evil one.
For Yours is the kingdom and the power
and the glory forever. Amen
(Matthew 6:9-13 NKJV).

"Your kingdom come. Your will be done on earth as it is in heaven." This prayer will bring the culture of Heaven to earth.

The Culture of Heaven

In Heaven, the word *crisis* has no meaning. In Heaven, every tear will be wiped from sorrowing eyes, and we will have no pain anymore (see Rev. 21:4). In Heaven, nobody will steal or cheat. Nobody will be fired from their jobs or foreclosed out of their homes. People will not take advantage of other people. Nobody will die anymore.

The culture of Heaven is not limited to "religion." The culture of Heaven includes everything:

1. The culture of Heaven has heavenly government.

2. The culture of Heaven has heavenly values.

3. The culture of Heaven has heavenly morals.

4. The culture of Heaven has heavenly economy.

5. The culture of Heaven has heavenly wealth.

6. The culture of Heaven has heavenly society.

Every time you are driven to your knees by the latest crisis, pray for the culture of the Kingdom of Heaven to come to earth a little bit more. Let your crisis propel you beyond the limitations of your present situation into new territory. Believe that there is more than one single way to solve any problem.

Crisis Compels the New and Different

Even if your progress has been halted by a seemingly impassable Red Sea, there is more than one way to get across it. You can try to swim. You can get a boat. Or God can work a miracle so you can walk across on dry ground—or how about on top of the waves? With the attitude of a Kingdom innovator, try to "walk on water," if that is what the King tells you to do. With Him, nothing is impossible!

Find new ways to solve old problems. That is how Kingdom people do it. Even Jesus never did the same miracle twice. He healed at least six different blind men. He touched the first two, who were healed together (see Matt. 9:27-31). He simply called another one, blind Bartimaeus, to come over to Him (see Mark 10:46-52). To heal another one, He cast a demon out (see Matt. 12:22; Luke 11:14). In another case, He put some of His saliva into the man's eyes and laid His hands on him (see Mark 8:22-26). With yet another man, He used His spit to make mud, put the mud on his blind eyes, and commanded him to wash in the Pool of Siloam (see John 9:1-41). Each of the blind men got healed. I don't think the success rate would have been so high if Jesus had stuck with Method Number One, the method that worked the first time, for every other situation.

If your problem is that you lost the only job you ever had and now you have no income, start thinking of new ways to solve your problem. Get some ideas from the Kingdom. Stop running your little depressed self around your default track: "No job…No money. Gotta get a job…Need a salary…Gotta get a job…Need a salary." What if there are no more jobs like your old one? Branch out. Look at more options. Never surrender to limitations.

Never be afraid to fail. Successful people are not afraid to fail. In fact, the way they got successful is by learning from their failures. Children are not afraid to fail, either. Trying and failing—and trying again—that is the way we learn and grow. When Jesus said He wanted His followers to become like little children, that is part of what He had in mind. (See Matthew 18:3-6; 19:14; Mark 10:14-15; Luke 18:16-17.)

Be willing to try anything once. When I was a teenager, the Holy Spirit said to me, "Look. Try it at least once. It is better to have tried and failed than not to have tried and not to know if you could have succeeded." At the same time, do not limit yourself to only one attempt. Maybe you tried the first time before the right season came. When the right time and season arrives, your effort can succeed.

At a certain point in Jesus' ministry, His brothers urged Him to "take His ministry public" by going to Jerusalem for the Feast of Tabernacles. Jesus said that the time was not yet right, and He stayed behind, but the very next morning, He made His way to Jerusalem:

> *Jesus told them, "The right time for Me has not yet come; for you any time is right....You go to the Feast. I am not yet going up to this Feast, because for Me the right time has not yet come." Having said this, He stayed in Galilee.*
>
> *However, after His brothers had left for the Feast, He went also, not publicly, but in secret* (John 7:6, 8-10).

His brothers would have objected to His way of doing things. Why would Jesus not go to the Feast on time? As He later told His disciples when He seemed to have delayed too long to visit His sick friend Lazarus, "Are there not twelve hours in the day?" (John 11:9 KJV). What He was saying is simply that you could be off by only 12 or 24 hours. Today could be the wrong day. Tomorrow could be the right day. In 12 or 24 hours, things could change. You could have tried something yesterday, and it failed, but today, you could try again, and it would succeed because the time is right. You could apply for a job and be told "No," but come back the next day and hear that something had opened up.

Remember that today's crisis is going away; it is seasonal and temporary. The Kingdom of Heaven is where you will find permanence. In your country, which is the Kingdom of God, everything has been secured permanently. Nothing gets lost in the Kingdom of Heaven.

From time to time, you should challenge your own success. Let's say you are *not* in any particular crisis at the moment. You are traveling down the highway of life, whistling a tune. Life is good. Well, that's not permanent, either, so you should prepare yourself mentally for changes. Do not be too surprised when the wheels fall off.

Get a head start on crisis. Before you lose your job, come up with something else. Think of things that nobody has ever done, and give them a try. That is how innovative Kingdom people think. I remember years ago when a woman came up to me after a Bible study. She had just gotten an idea for a business that had never been tried in the Bahamas. It doesn't sound too unusual now, but it was then. She had the idea to start a private mail-delivery company that would both pick up and deliver letters and packages to people's homes. She gave it a try, and it succeeded. Today, it is one of the largest mail-delivery companies in the country.

Communicate Kingdom culture by engaging the unknown. Take risks. Use your faith. Be courageous. Challenge conventions and buck traditional culture. Find new ways to do things; the conventional ways are not working. Remember what we said in the previous chapter about deployment versus employment? Maybe now is the time to start letting your work outpace your job.

Kingdom Lifestyle

Remember the keys of the Kingdom because they can become a lifestyle. One day, Jesus was explaining to His disciples why He spoke to the people in parables instead of like a news reporter. He told them, "The knowledge of the secrets of the kingdom of heaven has been given to you, but not to them" (Matt. 13:11).

We Kingdom people are the ones who can unlock the doors. We have the keys. The people of the world will never understand. When they come up against a locked door, they use all sorts of man-made keys, trying frantically to open the door. Meantime, Jesus is waiting for somebody to realize that this crisis of a locked door is just the right opportunity to slip in one of His keys. He said, "I will give you the keys of the kingdom of heaven; whatever you bind on earth will be bound in heaven, and whatever you loose on earth will be loosed in heaven" (Matt. 16:19).

All of the resources will be made available at exactly the right time. You will not improve your chances of getting the resources by anxiously worrying (see Matt. 6:31-34). You do not have to worry about getting a pink slip tomorrow. You do not have to worry about how you are going to pay the rent. Just live a trustful, righteous, Kingdom life and get your hand around those keys. Kingdom provisions lie behind the door of crisis.

May Your Kingdom come, Lord!

Endnote

1. Jon M. Huntsman, *Winners Never Cheat: Even in Difficult Times* (Upper Saddle River, NJ: Wharton School Publishing, 2009), 6.

CHAPTER 11

Ten Ways to Rise Above Crisis

Man is not imprisoned by habit. Great changes in him can be wrought by crisis—once that crisis can be recognized and understood.
          —Norman Cousins

"It was the best of times, it was the worst of times...." This immortal line appears at the very beginning of Charles Dickens' epic novel *A Tale of Two Cities*. The line gets quoted often, especially in times of great social upheaval and crisis—such as the time we are living through right now.

The enduring truth that Dickens' line captures is an underlying theme of this book. Crisis-filled times are also victory-filled times. With God's help, a person can rise above any crisis—and become better prepared to face the next one. I have been writing about this overcoming, rising-above process. Right here, right in the middle of your current crisis, is "where the rubber meets the road" in terms of your faith. A crisis will make you or break you. My mission is to make sure it *makes* you.

In this chapter, you will find ten approaches to your crisis situation of the moment. Some of these ways to rise above crisis will stand out to you more than others. They will just hit home somehow. That is because crises have seasons and stages. If your current crisis crashed into you only yesterday, you will be looking for a starting place. If you are somewhere in the middle of an ongoing crisis situation, you will need fortification of a different kind.

Whatever your circumstances and however you feel at this moment, I am sure that you will find something helpful in this chapter. Skim through these ten ways to rise above crisis to find the one you need to read first.

Number One: Initiate Solutions

In a crisis situation, you cannot wait to see what will happen. You cannot leave things up to somebody else.

Even if you are lying by the side of the road after a car accident and you cannot get up under your own power, the first thing you need to do is to pray and cry out for help. You need to take some kind of initiative. If you have been injured, you may have a long time of recovery ahead of you. Your whole life may be different. You will need to initiate further solutions as you go along.

You need to initiate solutions in order to get some control of an out-of-control situation just as you would if you were in a war zone and needed to retake territory under enemy occupation.

Just think of David and Goliath (see 1 Sam. 17). The Philistine army had caused a military crisis by bringing the giant, Goliath, to challenge the Israelites. Everybody was afraid of Goliath. Nobody thought they could win over such a formidable foe. But they *had* to, or they would be taken over by the Philistines. King Saul and his seasoned warriors were stalling for time.

Along came David, ostensibly to bring food to his big brothers, who were part of the army. He heard about Goliath's challenge, and he knew that something had to be done. With a combination of God-given courage and cleverness, David initiated a solution. He proposed that he himself, a young shepherd, should confront the giant. Was this some kind of a joke? How could a mere boy expect to succeed where well-armed warriors had failed?

The Israelite king was out of options, so he agreed to David's crazy plan. What did they have to lose? You know how it turned out. David was not crazy after all because he was not fighting on his own strength alone. Goliath was mocking him the whole time, but...

David said to the Philistine, "You come against me with sword and spear and javelin, but I come against you in the name of the Lord Almighty, the God of the armies of Israel, whom you have defied. This day the Lord will hand you over to me, and I'll strike you down and cut off your head. Today I will give the carcasses of the Philistine army to the birds of

*the air and the beasts of the earth, and the whole world will
know that there is a God in Israel. All those gathered here
will know that it is not by sword or spear that the Lord saves;
for the battle is the Lord's, and He will give all of you into
our hands"* (1 Samuel 17:45-47).

David used his trusty sling to throw one well-chosen,
well-aimed rock at Goliath. It could have just bounced off his
armor, but this one little stone stopped him dead, penetrating
his bare forehead. Goliath's huge body slammed to the dirt.
Then David "ran over and pulled Goliath's sword from its
sheath. David used it to kill the giant and cut off his head…"
(1 Sam. 17:51 NLT).

David took initiative—on his own—to address the crisis
that was threatening his nation. At any point, he could have
slipped away to go back home. Nobody was forcing him to
confront Goliath. In fact, the others were trying to persuade
him not to do it. David could have gone back to his father
and to tending his sheep, just waiting with crossed fingers for
more news from the battlefront. Instead, he risked his life,
and his bold initiative paid off.

Do you have some kind of a Goliath standing in your
way right now? Ask God to help you think of what to do.
Then initiate a solution to your problem. See if it works.
Adjust your plan, if necessary. Do not be afraid to try new
tactics. Do not retreat. Your initiative may prove to be the
answer to your problem.

Number Two: Place Demands on Your Potential

All of that initiative taking is going to place some demands on your potential. What I mean is that your actions are going to require you to draw on some gifts, some energy, and some qualities, such as courage, that you may have hidden inside you.

You may never have gotten to use those things before. You may have to look for them. But your search will be rewarded. You have more potential than you realize.

To help you locate the gifts and character qualities that you are going to need, you must overcome a number of possible hindrances, the enemies of your potential:

1. **Disobedience.** Look what happened to Jonah when God told him to go to Nineveh. His disobedience landed him in the belly of a fish.

2. **Sin.** At its root, sin is a declaration of independence from your Source, God. You cannot discover your potential without the help of the One who created you.

3. **Fear.** When you allow fear to rule you, you end up dwelling on what could go wrong rather than on what could go right. To tap into your potential, you must neutralize fear with faith.

4. **Discouragement.** God will not allow you to face a crisis that is too great for you to conquer. He will help. Discard discouragement and replace it with faith.

5. **Procrastination.** Do not drag your feet. There is no time like the present to get moving. "Don't sit there watching the wind. Do your own work. Don't stare at the clouds. Get on with your life" (Eccles. 11:4 TM).

6. **Past failures.** Refuse to be a "loser," no matter how many times you lose. Do not allow yourself to be paralyzed by memories of another time when an initiative failed.

7. **The opinions of others.** You are surrounded by naysayers who will tell you, "That idea will never work." Ask God what *He* thinks. His opinion is the only one that counts.

8. **Distractions.** Whatever does not help your progress hinders it. Obeying God too soon or too late is disobedience. Keep your focus. Do not let momentary urgencies deflect you.

9. **Success.** Do not get off the train if it stops at the station called "Success." An occasional success is a great encouragement, but you may not be at your destination yet.

10. **Tradition.** Move beyond "the way we've always done it" if you intend to overcome your time of crisis. There is always a better way. Dare to try something different.

11. **A wrong environment.** Carefully look at how you spend your time and energy and the people you

associate with. Is this atmosphere helping you to overcome your crisis situation?

12. **Comparison.** Avoid comparing yourself with others. Do not try to become someone else. Instead, aim to become the best possible *you*, making the most of your unique qualities.

13. **Opposition.** When (not if) you encounter roadblocks, do not turn back or camp out in the road. Do not compromise your plans, unless God tells you to do so.

14. **Pressure from society.** You may feel that you are swimming against the current. You may receive no encouragement at all. That does *not* mean you cannot succeed.

Every time you come up against a crisis situation, remember that you do have the right "stuff" inside. God planted it in you, and He may have allowed this crisis specifically in order to cause it to grow. Without delay, tap into your potential.

Number Three: Test the Creativity of Your Team

If you are working with other people, sit down with them and say, "OK, everybody. Let's find some new ways to think." If you can pull together a couple of friends, ask them to help you think of creative ways to overcome your crisis.

As God said after He had created Adam, "It is not good for the man to be alone" (Gen. 2:18). All of us need other people. Even if what you are facing seems to be a personal crisis only, you need what others have to offer. If what you are facing is a corporate crisis, you need other people still more.

Do you remember the story of Nehemiah? He lived in exile in Babylon, far away from his native land, and when he heard that the walls of Jerusalem were in ruins, he wanted to do something about it. (See Nehemiah 1–5.) Nehemiah loved his city, and he loved its people. The vulnerable and shameful state of the city was enough of a crisis to Nehemiah that he was willing to dedicate years of his life to rebuild it. In order to undertake such a massive project, he needed the help of hundreds of people, from King Artaxerxes of Babylon on down to the most humble Israelite laborer in Jerusalem.

In the midst of the project, he needed to rally the people. They were under great opposition from their enemies, and they could hardly work anymore. Nehemiah pulled them together and told them to try something new. From that time on, half of the laborers worked at wall-building while the other half stood guard with their weapons (see Neh. 4). This was not the ordinary way to build a city wall. Nehemiah's creative solution worked. The wall was completed, and Jerusalem once again was surrounded with protection.

Number Four: Believe in Your Ability to Solve Problems

You must believe that you have the capacity to solve the problems you are facing. After all, you are a child of the King, and He can supply you with anything you may be lacking. Your ability to solve problems stems from His unlimited ability to solve problems.

As a child of the King, your Kingdom supply flows through your righteousness. Righteousness attracts God. He is righteous, and He has made it possible for us to reflect His righteousness.

Righteousness is the "scepter of His Kingdom" (see Heb. 1:8). A scepter is the symbol of authority for a king. When an ancient king extended his scepter toward a person, the person came under his favor and blessing. When the King of kings extends His scepter of righteousness over you, you come under His protection and provision. Because of His favor, you are rich; you lack nothing. Certainly you have the ability to solve problems. That comes with your status as His special child.

The Bible tells us that the way to tap into God's Kingdom supply is by maintaining a righteous life. We cannot do it perfectly—that's what repentance is for—and we cannot do it on our own—that's why we have been given His Holy Spirit—but we can have full confidence that we have access to His provision when we carry the key of righteousness. Remember, again, what Jesus said: "But seek first His kingdom and His righteousness, and all these things will be given to you as well" (Matt. 6:33).

If we fail to commit ourselves to a life of righteousness, we will never share in the riches of the Kingdom. The riches of the Kingdom include wisdom, discernment, and understanding. Your ability to rise above a crisis and to solve pressing problems depends upon your maturity in Him. You know that this is true from your own personal experience.

So believe in your ability to solve the problems engendered by your current crisis—just as much as you believe in His ability to save you and supply you with an abundance of whatever you need.

Number Five: Look at What You Have, Not What You Don't Have

You will remember back in Chapter 4 ("Seven Ways to Manage a Crisis") that my first two points were (1) Determine what your needs are, and (2) Acquire only what you need. When you want to rise above a crisis, especially a financial crisis, you need to look at what you have already, determine how to use it, and stop fretting about what you do not have, especially if what you do not have is some luxury item, not something you truly *need*.

In particular, stop comparing yourself to others. If they seem to be recession-proof, so what? Do not compromise your righteousness by falling into jealousy or envy or bitterness. Do not let anxiety cause you to become dishonest or grasping.

Do not blame "the system" for your difficulties. Even if the worldly culture around you has caused genuine suffering in your life, you are not subject to the worldly system; you are a subject in the Kingdom of Heaven. You know how to ask the King for whatever you need, asking according to His will. You can hear Him, and you can obey Him. "…If we ask anything according to His will, He hears us. And if we know that He hears us—whatever we ask—we know that we have what we asked of Him" (1 John 5:14-15).

Start by simply looking at what you have, and ask God to help you work with that.

Number Six: Study What You Have

When Jesus' disciples told Him about the food crisis they had—more than 5,000 people needed a meal—what did Jesus ask them? He said, "How many loaves do you have?" (See Matthew 15:34 and Mark 6:38.) Starting with what they had, a few loaves of bread and a few fish, Jesus multiplied enough food for everyone. What they had already was enough for Him to use. They had more than enough. Miraculously, they rose above the crisis of the moment.

So what do you have? Study it and bring it to Him. Study your possessions. Study your experience. Study your relationships. Until you bring what you have to Him, He cannot use it.

When Joseph was in prison, he did not have much. But he took what he had—his ability to interpret dreams, his ability to work hard, and his limited relationships—and God turned them into freedom and more. Joseph had relationships with the baker and the cupbearer (see Gen. 40). As it turned out, one of those relationships was a very important one to have.

Number Seven: Look for the Potential of Your Resources

By studying what you have, you can look at it with fresh eyes. Even if it seems to be very limited at first, you can discover the potential uses of what you have.

God created you to be a Kingdom-bringer, someone who is supposed to manage a piece of the Kingdom of God on earth. He did not give you religious rules and regulations. He gave you resources. He gave Adam a domain, and He has given you a domain as well.

Your territory of dominion may or may not include actual land. It includes whatever you have a legal right over, in Kingdom terms. Your legal rulership is by privilege and delegation because of your relationship with the King.

To make it possible for you to carry out the management mandate that started with Adam, not only will the King multiply your resources whenever He needs to, He will show you the hidden potential in the resources you already have. With the widow in Zarephath, the resources she already had were very limited indeed. All she had was a jar with one small handful of flour in it and a jug with a little bit of oil left in the bottom. (See First Kings 17:7-16.) That wasn't much for Elijah's God to work with. But what potential it had! Every day, Elijah had supper with the widow and her son, and every day some more food came from that meager supply.

I have seen a widow near the airport in Nassau who has found the potential of one of her primary resources, which is her car. She drives it to wherever construction crews are working, and she sells lunches and snacks to the workers out of the trunk of her car. She has put three of her children through school by making the most of her limited resources. She saw the potential of an empty car trunk and her ability to prepare good-tasting food.

What are your resources? What is the *potential* of your resources?

Number Eight: See Beyond the Norm

You have got to get used to keeping your eyes wide open. A crisis is a wonderful time to learn to see beyond the normal human culture you live in. Seeing beyond the norm involves laying hold of Kingdom principles. It involves rediscovering the Kingdom of God.

Living as part of the Kingdom of God is quite different from your everyday, non-Kingdom existence. The Kingdom of God is "beyond the norm." In the Kingdom of Heaven, here is what is considered normal:

1. The King is sovereign. He is the Creator, and He is in charge of everything, everywhere.

2. This King chooses His citizens. Citizenship in the Kingdom is a privilege.

3. This King is the Source of all delegated authority, and He delegates authority to His subjects.

4. This King governs His Kingdom with complete righteousness.

5. He conveys His will, intents, desires, and purposes to His citizens.

6. The King wants His people to know His will and to obey Him.

7. He speaks to His citizens through His written Word and directly to their spirits through His Holy Spirit.

8. The King's will, intents, desires, and purposes are expressed through His principles, precepts, laws, and systems.

9. He maintains a code of conduct.

10. He enables His subjects to attain His values and moral standards.

11. The culture of the Kingdom of Heaven is expressed through its citizenry, which is the Church.

12. The culture of the Kingdom is manifested in its citizens' language, dress, eating habits, values, morals, and sense of self-worth.

13. The Kingdom is a "commonwealth," which means that the King shares His resources.

14. The Kingdom is not a welfare state. Its flourishing economy depends upon the hard work of its citizens.

15. The King protects His citizens with an angelic army.

16. The King educates His citizens. He wants to make sure that they remember what the Kingdom of Heaven is like.

17. The Kingdom of Heaven is filled with light and glory. The righteousness and compassion and generosity of the King are everywhere.

18. The citizens of the Kingdom learn obedience through the trials and crises that the King allows.

19. The citizens of the Kingdom worship the King with awe and gratitude.

20. The citizens of the Kingdom help the King to expand the Kingdom territory as they exercise the authority He has delegated to them.

See beyond the norm. The world around you is not the norm; the Kingdom of God is.

Number Nine: Understand the True Nature of Resources

You need to understand what your God-given resources are. Only some of them are actual, physical possessions. Other resources include your giftings and your character traits. Another resource is time. One of your most important resources is your faith.

As Jesus said, "Your life consists of more than your possessions" (see Matt. 6:25). Taken together, all of your resources must be managed well in order for you to flourish. How you manage and invest your resources determines your future resources. God is watching to see how well you manage what He has given you already, before He will give you additional resources. He allows problems and crises to occur to test your resource-management ability.

In God's Kingdom, an important part of management ability is generosity. Are you willing to tithe—and more? Are you willing to humble yourself and work hard, modeling yourself after your servant-King?

Because good management involves adding value to whatever is being managed, you need to invest your energy and gifts well. If you understand the true nature of resources, you will also appreciate their true value.

Number Ten: Act on Faith

You can talk about the Kingdom all day, and you can talk about things like God's management mandate. But unless you step out and *do* something, it is not good for much. You need to act. Nobody ever overcame a crisis by sitting down and doing nothing.

You know how the Old Testament is filled with stories about good kings and bad kings. After Israel got started having kings, it was a constant stream: good/bad/good/bad…. A righteous king would be followed by his son, who was an evil man with a wicked agenda, and vice versa. Some of those kings were really bad news; they were crisis-makers.

Others, though, were considered good because they reflected godly qualities, and they promoted godly principles. Time and time again, the good kings pulled the kingdoms of Israel and Judah back to their true King, God. When the good kings were on the throne, problems and crisis could be solved swiftly with God's help.

Those Old Testament books of Kings and Chronicles could be called the Books of Crisis. It seems as if one crisis is barely averted and its repercussions silenced before another comes up to replace it. The kings, and the people under them, had to stay ready for the next blow to fall. Then, as today, cultures were clashing, and human ambitions and greed were making life miserable.

A leader who would step out and act on faith in obedience to God's will was one who could win over his enemies. King David was the foremost of the good kings, and his victories over enemy forces are still celebrated in God-glorifying song:

The Lord is my rock, my fortress and my deliverer;
> *my God is my rock, in whom I take refuge,*
> *my shield and the horn of my salvation.*

He is my stronghold, my refuge and my savior—
> *from violent men You save me.*

I call to the Lord, who is worthy of praise,
> *and I am saved from my enemies.*

The waves of death swirled about me;
> *the torrents of destruction overwhelmed me....*

In my distress I called to the Lord....

He shot arrows and scattered the enemies,
> *bolts of lightning and routed them....*

He reached down from on high and took hold of me;
> *He drew me out of deep waters.*

He rescued me from my powerful enemy,
> *from my foes, who were too strong for me.*

They confronted me in the day of my disaster,
    but the Lord was my support.

He brought me out into a spacious place;
    He rescued me because He delighted in me.

The Lord has dealt with me according to my righteousness;
    according to the cleanness of my hands He has
    rewarded me.

For I have kept the ways of the Lord;
    I have not done evil by turning from my God....

You save the humble,
    but Your eyes are on the haughty to bring them
    low.

You are my lamp, O Lord;
    the Lord turns my darkness into light.

With Your help I can advance against a troop;
    with my God I can scale a wall.

As for God, His way is perfect;
    the word of the Lord is flawless.

He is a shield
    for all who take refuge in Him.

For who is God besides the Lord?
    And who is the Rock except our God?

It is God who arms me with strength
    and makes my way perfect.

He makes my feet like the feet of a deer;
    He enables me to stand on the heights.

He trains my hands for battle;
my arms can bend a bow of bronze.

You give me Your shield of victory;
You stoop down to make me great.

You broaden the path beneath me,
so that my ankles do not turn.

I pursued my enemies and crushed them;
I did not turn back till they were destroyed....

The Lord lives! Praise be to my Rock!
Exalted be God, the Rock, my Savior!

...who sets me free from my enemies.
You exalted me above my foes;
from violent men You rescued me.

Therefore I will praise You, O Lord, among the nations;
I will sing praises to Your name.

He gives His king great victories...(2 Samuel 22:2-5,7,15,17-22,28-38,47,49-51).

Becoming an Overcomer

As I have been in the process of writing this book, the worldwide financial crisis has been getting worse every day. You and I know that this is going to be a long haul. We are going to need the principles and wisdom contained in this book because each one of us will be facing new crises in the coming months and years.

As I have been saying since the beginning, no one is exempt from crisis, not even the most righteous believer in the Kingdom of God. But the Kingdom of God itself is never in crisis. As citizens of that Kingdom, we need to make it our business to tackle every crisis situation in faith, knowing that part of the reason God allows and even sends crises is to enable us to grow.

He wants us to grow into His image in every way, reflecting His Kingdom culture to the messy world we live in. He wants us to be part of the solution in each worldly crisis we face, not part of the problem. He wants us to import His Kingdom culture by living by its principles and by keeping in active communication with its King.

Crises are always going to be part of the equation of life on earth until Jesus comes again. The question for you is, how will you handle your next crisis? Will you demonstrate the right combination of faith, stability, management ability, perseverance, and confidence in the gifts He has given you?

Will you rise to the challenge?

I want to leave you with a challenge of my own. Here it is: this book represents your instructions for the next six months to five years. I want you to take the advice I have given you and make it part of your "default response" to the crises you will surely face. My challenge is simple: Meet me on the other side of your crisis. I will be there ahead of you, waiting for you!

Bahamas Faith Ministries International

The Diplomat Centre
Carmichael Road
P.O. Box N-9583
Nassau, Bahamas

Tel: 242-341-6444
Fax: 242-361-2260

Web site: http://www.bfmmm.com.

Additional copies of this book and other
book titles from DESTINY IMAGE are
available at your local bookstore.

Call toll-free: 1-800-722-6774.

Send a request for a catalog to:

Destiny Image® Publishers, Inc.
P.O. Box 310
Shippensburg, PA 17257-0310

*"Speaking to the Purposes of God for This
Generation and for the Generations to Come."*

**For a complete list of our titles,
visit us at www.destinyimage.com.**